75 Flowers
for Cake Decorators

75 Flowers
for Cake Decorators

Helen Penman

U.S. consultant: Dianne Gruenberg

ST. MARTIN'S GRIFFIN
NEW YORK

A QUARTO BOOK

75 Flowers for Cake Decorators

Copyright © 2014 Quarto Inc.

Printed in China. For information, address

St. Martin's Press, 175 Fifth Avenue,

New York, N.Y. 10010.

5330 5297 3/14

www.stmartins.com

Library of Congress Cataloging-in-Publication

Data Available Upon Request

ISBN: 978-1-250-04484-6

First US Edition: March 2014

QUAR.HFFC

Conceived, designed, and produced by:

Quarto Publishing plc

The Old Brewery

6 Blundell Street

London N7 9BH

Senior Editor: Ruth Patrick
Art Editor and Designer: Emma Clayton
Photographer: Phil Wilkins
Proofreader: Sarah Hoggett
Indexer: Helen Snaith
Picture Researcher: Sarah Bell
Art Director: Caroline Guest

Creative Director: Moira Clinch
Publisher: Paul Carslake

Color separation by Cypress Colours (HK) Ltd

Printed by 1010 Printing International

Ltd, China

9 8 7 6 5 4 3 2 1

Contents

Foreword

I have always loved flower making, so it was a real privilege to be offered the opportunity to write a book on the subject. Trying to decide which flowers to include was not easy though, and hopefully there is a flower for everyone. I wanted to show the traditional flowers along with the more unusual ones. I also wanted to include groups of flowers that would go well together on a cake—for example, the Summer flowers cake (see pages 34–35) looks impressive but is easily manageable with a little experience.

I started making cakes almost 20 years ago. I had commissioned a cake for my father's birthday, and when it came it was such poor quality that I decided I could do better myself. I got books from the library and tried things out. I enrolled at City of Bath College, UK, and took a City & Guilds course with Stephen Benison, and I now run my own cake decorating business, Too Nice To Slice. I do hope you enjoy making the flowers in this book, and I hope to write more for you in the future!

Helen

Helen Penman

About This Book

This book starts with tools and materials, recipes, and techniques, and is followed by a comprehensive directory of flowers, organized by the material from which they are made.

Techniques (pages 14–31)

Core techniques to learn before you embark on making the flowers. Here you will find recipes for all the pastes, should you wish to make your own, and techniques for piping and using buttercream, fondant, and marzipan. There is also a brief introduction to the skills you will need to make flowers.

Core information is given in the introduction to each technique.

Photo steps show the technique.

Templates (pages 136–139)

Many of the leaf and petal cutters used for the flowers are represented here as templates for you to trace or scan and cut out.

Flower directory (pages 32–135)

There are 75 flowers for you to select from in a range of materials—chocolate, marzipan, gum paste, buttercream, and royal icing. One or two classic flowers—roses and lilies, for example—are demonstrated in more than one material.

Parts of this flower are inedible. Flag indicates the flowers that have inedible components, such as wire or cotton stamens.

Flagged by skill level on a scale from easy to advanced.

Written text explains the making process.

Here and there, large-scale celebration cakes are used to display the flowers.

Tools and materials listing. Basic tool kits are explained on page 14. The list includes tools and materials, including quantities of paste and how many flowers the quantity of material makes: this is always given as an approximation.

The development of the flower is shown in stages.

Flower Selector

On these pages you will find all the flowers featured in the book. Browse the selector to find the flower or flowers that would work best on the cake or cupcake you have in mind, then turn to the instructions on the referenced page.

page 41

page 42

page 43

page 44

page 46

page 47

page 48

page 50

page 51

page 52

page 53

page 54

page 55

page 56

page 58

page 59

page 60

page 62

page 63

page 65

page 68

page 66

000

page 72

page 69

page 70

page 71

page 74

page 75

page 77

page 78

page 80

page 81

page 82

page 84

page 85

page 86

page 88

page 89

page 90

page 92

page 93

page 94

page 96

page 97

page 100

page 102

page 103

page 98

page 104

page 106

page 108

page 111

page 112

page 113

page 114

page 115

page 116

page 117

page 118

page 119

page 120

page 121

page 122

page 123

page 124

page 125

page 127

page 128

page 129

page 130

page 131

page 132

page 133

page 134

page 135

Tools and Materials

Basic Tool Kit: Chocolate
- Work board
- Foam pad
- Plastic sheets x 2
- Rolling pin
- X-acto knife
- Bone tool
- Ball tool
- Flower veining tool
- Toothpick
- Paintbrush
- Water brush

Basic Tool Kit: Marzipan
- Work board
- Foam pad
- Plastic sheets x 2
- Rolling pin
- X-acto knife
- Bone tool
- Flower veining tool
- Toothpick
- Paintbrush
- Water brush

Basic Tool Kit: Gum paste
- Work board
- Foam pad
- Plastic sheets x 2
- Rolling pin
- X-acto knife
- Flower veining tool
- Paintbrush
- Water brush
- Former

Basic tool kits

Work board
An acrylic work board is the perfect surface to roll out paste or chocolate; it is easily washable and offers a blemish-free surface.

Foam pad
The foam pad is specially made for flower making. It is firm but soft, and has a non-stick surface. Some foam pad models have holes to support particular shapes, like Mexican hats.

Plastic sheet
To get the best from modeling chocolate or marzipan, roll out between two plastic sheets; this reduces the need to handle the paste too much, which will soften and start to melt in the case of chocolate. The sheets should be washed and dried after use.

Rolling pin
Rolling pins are available in many sizes and made of various materials. They can be textured to give different effects on the rolled-out paste, but for basic flower making a short length made from acrylic works best. A longer acrylic pin is required to roll out fondant for covering cakes.

X-acto knife
The X-acto knife is a sharp, smooth, stainless-steel blade—great for cutting pastes.

Bone tool
Used to smooth curves in fondant when modeling and to frill petals in flower making, it is also used to soften and thin the edges of leaves and flowers.

Ball tool
This tool has many of the same features as the bone tool, having a large and small ball at each end of the handle. The ball tool will soften and cup petals without tearing the delicate paste.

Flower veining tool
The flower veining tool or Dresden tool is used to smooth and flute paste, using the back of the tool. It is also ideal for creating finely detailed veins on leaves and flowers.

Toothpick
The toothpick has three uses— to support a flower while it is drying, as a texturing/frilling tool, and to add color from a paste pot to the medium.

Paintbrush
Paintbrushes should include a broad one for dusting flowers and one that has fine bristles to allow for detailed and accurate painting.

Water brush
A water brush is a paintbrush with its own water reservoir contained within the brush. Clean the brush and change the water regularly.

Former
A former is any support for a flower, petal, or leaf while it is drying. The device may be store-bought, with cups for drying curved shapes or spaces for hanging flowers, or it may be improvised with paper towels rolled into elongated sausage shapes.

General tools

Palette knife
A palette knife is a flat-bladed knife, with either a straight or an angled handle. This knife comes in several sizes, from very small to assist in lifting delicate items onto a cake to extra large to smooth soft paste such as buttercream over cakes and cupcakes.

Piping bag
The piping bag is specifically designed to hold a soft medium such as buttercream, royal icing, or jam. It is usually used in conjunction with a piping tip.

Decorating tip
This is a stainless-steel cone-shaped tube with ends of different designs that texture the soft medium as it is being piped. Use with a piping bag. When the medium is extruded through the tip, it takes on the shape of the tip, holding that shape to create attractive finishes to cakes and cupcakes.

Every sugarcrafter has their favorite tools for making flowers. Several tools will do more than one job and there are some that are indispensable. When buying tools, buy the best you can afford. There are also general kitchen tools that are useful when making flowers.

Cutters come in many shapes.

Cutters

Flower and leaf cutters are made of stainless steel, so they keep their shape well, are easy to clean, and the edge does not blunt quickly. The cutter will be shaped to emulate the flower/ leaf/petal that is being made, and there are hundreds to choose from in various sizes, depending on the size of flower being made.

Pizza cutter

This tool is perfect to use for long sections of paste requiring trimming, because it cuts without tearing the paste.

Molds

Molds save time, as they will shape a piece of paste quickly without the need to model or sculpt. These are excellent if you are short of time or a beginner, but they can be expensive.

Veiners

Veiners are usually made from soft material that is food safe and non-stick. They generally come in two sides so the petal/leaf is veined on both sides at the same time. Veiners vary in price depending on the quality of the veining, some made to be a true representation of that particular petal or leaf while others are more impressionistic.

Templates

Templates are a quick solution to the lack of a specific cutter. Make them from stiff card and cut around using a pizza cutter or scalpel.

Celstick

A non-stick nylon stick, similar to a toothpick and approved for use with food. The Celstick works in a similar way to a toothpick for thinning and frilling without the risk of it sticking to the paste and tearing the petal or leaf.

Materials

Food-grade wire

Cake decorating and sugarcraft flower wires are available in standard lengths of 12 in. (30.5 cm) and various gauges (thicknesses) and colors. They are inedible.

Stamens

Stamens are made from cotton specifically for making sugar flowers more lifelike. They come in an array of colors, shapes, and sizes to suit whatever flower is being made. Cotton stamens are inedible. Edible stamens can be made as an alternative.

Posy picks

A posy pick is a small, hollow cone made of food-grade plastic. The pick is inserted into a cake or cupcake so that wired flowers can be used to decorate the cake without the wires or floral tape coming into contact with the cake. The non-edible wired flowers and the pick can be easily removed before the cake is eaten.

Floral tape

This is a paper-and-latex tape used to bind flower wires. It is available in various shades of green, red, brown, and white. To create a narrower tape, cut the strip into three (see page 31). Dust white tape with petal dust color to complement the flower. Floral tape is inedible and should not come into contact with the cake or cupcake.

Pollen powder

Pollen powder is a granular food color ideal for coloring stamen heads and creating a textured effect on icing. Simply shake pollen powder over the moistened article or surface. Pollen powder gives a lifelike pollen effect to stamens. If this is not available, an effective solution is to use semolina with petal dust added.

Food colors

Powder food color is used when you don't want to alter the consistency of the medium. This is important when using modeling chocolate or marzipan where a liquid-based color would make the paste more sticky and unworkable. Use liquid, gel, or paste food color when the medium will not alter significantly by the introduction of extra liquid. These food colors will give a deeper color than can be achieved with powder.

Petal dust color

Petal dust or powder color is available in an enormous range of shades. The petal dust can be used to color paste—either because you want a light shade, or because the medium warrants the use of powder—or it can be dusted on a finished piece. Some dusts have special effects added such as glitter that enhances the appearance.

Cocoa butter

Cocoa butter is a hard, pale yellow edible vegetable fat extracted from the cocoa bean. It is used to make chocolate, but also as a base for painting on cakes, cupcakes, and chocolate flowers. It has a low melting point so melts easily over heated water. Melted cocoa butter blends well with petal dusts to create paint.

From left: paint brushes, flower veining tool, ball tool, and bone tool.

Basic Recipes

The pastes used in this book are easily found in local grocery stores or specialist cake-decorating outlets. However, if you want to make them yourself, you will find all the recipes you need on the following pages.

Fondant

Fondant is a cake covering that rolls out smoothly. It is a sweet paste that sets firmly on the outside, but is still soft enough to cut with a knife. It can easily be colored using a paste or liquid color.

Ingredients

Makes 2 lb 4 oz (1 kg)
- 4 tbsp cold water
- 4 tsp/1 sachet powdered gelatin (you can use the vegetarian version if you prefer)
- 4 fl oz (125 ml) liquid glucose
- 1 tbsp glycerine
- 2¼ lb (1 kg) confectioner's sugar

1 Place the cold water in a bowl, sprinkle the gelatin over, and then soak until spongy.

2 Stand the bowl over a pan of hot but not boiling water and stir until the gelatin has dissolved.

3 Add the glucose and glycerine, stirring until well blended and runny.

4 Sift the confectioner's sugar into a large bowl. Make a well in the center and slowly pour in the liquid ingredients, stirring constantly.

5 Mix well, then turn out onto a surface dusted with confectioner's sugar. Knead until smooth, sprinkling with extra confectioner's sugar if the paste becomes excessively sticky.

6 The fondant can be used straight away or wrapped and stored in a plastic bag until needed.

Fondant cake covering with gum paste flowers.

Marzipan

Marzipan is a grainy paste. This is a delicious and straightforward marzipan recipe that can be given different flavors with the addition of cinnamon or orange zest. Try a touch of brandy for a special flavoring during the holiday season.

Ingredients

Makes 1 lb 2 oz (500 g)
- 9 oz (250 g) confectioner's sugar
- 9 oz (250 g) finely ground blanched almonds
- 2 egg whites
- ½ tsp salt
- ½ tsp almond extract

1 Sift all the dry ingredients together, add the egg whites and almond extract, and mix with a wooden spoon.

2 Store in a sealed bag overnight in the fridge.

Gum paste

Gum paste is a firm paste used for making flowers that need support. It has gum tragacanth added. If you don't want to make the whole paste from scratch, you could add 1 tsp to ½ lb (250g) fondant and this will give you a workable paste in three hours.

Ingredients

Makes 1 lb 2 oz (500 g)
- 1 lb 2 oz (500 g) confectioner's sugar
- 1 tbsp gum tragacanth
- 1½ tbsp cold water
- 2 tsp powdered gelatin
- 2 tsp liquid glucose
- 1 tbsp white shortening
- 1 medium egg white

1 Sift the confectioner's sugar and gum tragacanth into the mixing bowl of a heavy-duty mixer.

2 Put the water in a bowl, sprinkle the gelatin over, and soak until spongy. Stand the bowl over a pan of hot water and stir until the gelatin has dissolved.

4 Add the glucose and white shortening to the gelatin, stirring until all the ingredients are melted and mixed.

5 Add the mixture to the confectioner's sugar, along with the egg white. Beat the mixture very slowly—it will look a dark cream color at this stage, due to the gelatin.

7 Increase the speed to maximum until the paste becomes white and stretchy.

8 Grease your hands and remove the paste from the bowl. Pull and stretch the paste, then knead together. Place in a plastic bag and store in an airtight container. Leave the paste to mature for at least 24 hours.

Modeling chocolate

Modeling chocolate can be made using milk or dark chocolate; however, to be able to color modeling chocolate, you will need to work with a base of white modeling chocolate. Always use powder color with modeling chocolate, since liquid color will make the paste too sticky and unworkable.

Ingredients

Makes 1 lb 2 oz (500 g)
- 12 oz (350 g) white chocolate chips
- 125ml (4 fl oz) corn syrup or liquid glucose

1 Melt the chocolate slowly in the microwave, giving it blasts of 10–20 seconds at a time until it is all melted. Alternatively, melt in a bowl held over a pan of hot water. Stir well to distribute the heat throughout the whole of the melted chocolate.

2 Warm up the corn syrup so that, when the two mix together, the syrup doesn't cool the chocolate.

3 Blend the two together, then pour onto plastic wrap. Cover with the plastic wrap and leave to cool for two to three hours.

4 Once cool, knead until smooth, then place in a sealed bag until required.

Buttercream

Buttercream is a delicious, fluffy icing that is used as a filling or topping for cupcakes and cakes. Buttercream is versatile and can be piped into delicious flower decorations that are tasty and wonderful to look at. Buttercream becomes crispy on the outside but still soft and creamy inside.

The consistency needs to be firmer for flower piping, so less milk will be required, but a thinner buttercream is ideal for a crumb coat on a cake. The flavor of the buttercream can be altered by adding different extracts, such as peppermint, lemon, coconut, or coffee, and the color can be changed using food paste colors. If you want a light-colored icing, use only clear flavorings, but remember that darker colors will deepen on setting. The addition of cocoa powder to the finished buttercream will make a delicious chocolate buttercream.

Buttercream is affected by heat and humidity—buttercreamed cakes can be left for three to four days at room temperature, but high temperature will cause buttercream to soften and melt. Don't be tempted to refrigerate, as this will cause condensation on the icing and colors will bleed.

Ingredients

Makes 1 lb 14 oz (850 g)

- 4½ oz (125 g) softened butter
- 4½ oz (125 g) white vegetable shortening
- 1 lb 5 oz (600 g) confectioner's sugar
- 1 tsp vanilla extract
- Milk (optional depending on consistency)

Plain buttercream

Combine the ingredients in a large bowl, and beat on a low speed until well blended or hand mix with a wooden spoon. Continue for five minutes until creamy. Keep the icing covered to prevent the icing from drying and becoming crispy. The buttercream can be kept in the refrigerator for up to six weeks—rebeat it before using.

Two-tone buttercream—method 1

1 Prepare the buttercream.

2 Using paste food color, paint a streak up one side of the piping bag, then fill the bag with buttercream using a palette knife.

3 Start piping and the paste color will color the buttercream as it is squeezed out.

Two-tone buttercream—method 2

1 Prepare the buttercream.

2 Split into two batches and color each to suit the theme of your cake or cupcake.

3 Fill one side of the piping bag with one color and fill the other side with the other color.

4 Start piping and the two colors will come through the tip.

Royal icing

Royal icing can be used to cover a cake, secure decorations onto a cake, or pipe designs or sugar flowers. When using royal icing as a cake covering, the addition of glycerine to the recipe is important, as this will stop the icing from drying too hard and making it impossible to slice.

There are many different recipes for royal icing; traditionally, raw egg whites were used. Now, meringue powder takes the place of raw egg white. If you are in a hurry, royal icing powder is now also widely available—it is quick to make up with the addition of water—or a ready-made royal icing can also be bought.

Ingredients

Makes 1 lb (450 g)

- 1 lb (450 g) sifted confectioner's sugar
- 3 level tbsp meringue powder
- ½ tsp cream of tartar
- 5–6 tbsp lukewarm water

1 Firstly, ensure that all utensils are free from grease.

2 Sift the confectioner's sugar into a clean metallic bowl using a fine sifter (this avoids large granules of confectioner's sugar getting into the mix and clogging the decorating tip) and pour in the meringue powder and water.

3 Whisk gently, then add the cream of tartar, slowly increasing the speed of the mixer or beating with a metal spoon or palette knife.

4 Beat on high speed until the icing is glossy and forms stiff peaks when the whisk is lifted from the icing, or beat with a metal spoon or palette knife.

5 Royal icing will dry quickly and form a crust, which makes it impossible to pipe without clogging up the decorating tip. So when using royal icing, cover the surface of the icing with a lightly dampened piece of paper towel. This will stop the crust from forming and ensure that there is no wastage. The icing can be stored in an airtight container for up to two weeks in the refrigerator. Always rebeat before use. Flowers made using royal icing can be stored in an airtight container for several months.

Piping techniques

The techniques in this book for piping with royal icing or buttercream are the same, so if you prefer to pipe a flower in royal icing but the instructions are for buttercream, you can easily use royal icing and the results will be as good! If you have previously been piping with buttercream, you will need to meticulously wash your equipment to remove the grease before using royal icing.

When using royal icing to pipe flowers, some will require a softer consistency of icing than others, giving a different texture when piped. A stiffer icing will suit flowers with rough edges such as the carnation (see page 113) or the rose (see page 112), but again the rose can be made with a softer icing to create a different flower.

Basic Techniques

Making a piping bag

Ready-made piping bags in either plastic, polyester, or silicone can be bought and are great time savers, although they can be costly. The cloth bags can be washed several times and reused, and are ideal for large quantities. Piping bags can be made from flat, square sheets of parchment paper and of any size suitable to the need for the bag, although for large quantities of buttercream, a plastic or cloth bag will be easier to use.

Filling and covering a cake with buttercream

A cake can be filled and completely covered with buttercream as the decorative finish; alternatively buttercream can be used as a sticking agent if the cake is to be finished in fondant. If the cake is going to be completely finished with buttercream, it is better to cover it first with a thin layer of buttercream as a crumb coat, place in the refrigerator for 20 minutes, and then cover the cake with the final layer of buttercream without the worry that crumbs will get into it and spoil the finished covering. If you prefer you can pipe the buttercream, creating a patterned finish to the cake, rather than applying with a palette knife.

1 Always make the parchment bag using a double layer of paper because the paper gets rather soft. Take a square of paper and fold it in half to create a triangle.

2 Take the two points at either end of the long side and twist them over each other to form a cone, with the third point being at the top of the cone.

1 Slice the cake in half and fill the cake with buttercream—add a jam filling also, if you wish. Place the top layer of cake on top and press together.

2 Apply a thin layer of buttercream over the whole of the cake as a crumb coat, then place in the refrigerator for 20 minutes.

3 Fold the top over to secure the paper in place.

4 Snip off the end of the point and insert the appropriate decorating tip.

3 Cover the whole cake with softened buttercream, using a palette knife to spread a thick, smooth layer over the whole of the side of the cake.

4 Use a buttercream comb to create textures on the side of the cake or, if you prefer, stick shredded coconut, chocolate chips, curls, nuts, etc. to the side of the cake.

Filling cupcakes

Cupcakes are delicious morsels of sponge cake wrapped in a paper case. Traditionally, cupcakes were covered with buttercream or the center cut out and filled with buttercream and the center popped back on top. Cupcakes can be filled with jam using a decorating tip, then topped with buttercream (see right).

1 Place the decorating tip in the bottom of the piping bag. If you are using a tube with a relatively small hole, you may want to sift the jam first to remove any lumps that might get stuck. If the tube has a large end, sifting is not necessary.

2 Fill the bag with jam, then push it into the top of the cupcake and squeeze a small amount of jam into the cupcake.

Covering cupcakes with buttercream

Buttercream can be piped onto cupcakes to give a decorative finish—a quick and simple way to create a delightful topping. Alternatively, the piping can be used as a base for further decoration. Or the buttercream can be applied to the top of the cupcake using a palette knife. The cupcakes can then be decorated with flowers. If piping, place a star decorating tip into the piping bag. The bag needs to be of a large size to accommodate a sufficient amount of buttercream—there is nothing more annoying than trying to refill the bag. Fill the bag three-quarters full of buttercream, fold over the top, and you are ready to pipe.

Piping up to a point

Start by piping around the edge of the cupcake, working inward and upward with successive layers, and finishing with a point.

Piping flat

Start by piping in the center of the cupcake, working around in a spiral fashion to the edge of the cake.

Applying with a palette knife

Take a dessert spoon of buttercream and, using a flat palette knife, spread liberally over the top of the cake.

Ruffled effect

Work from left to right on the cupcake and pipe in lines, working backward and forward to give a ruffled appearance.

Mini swirls

Pipe "dots" of buttercream over the top of the cupcake with a star decorating tip, completely covering it for a swirly appearance.

Covering cupcakes with fondant

Covering cupcakes in rolled fondant leaves a smooth, crisp finish, which can be embossed or crimped to add feature—but take care to roll quite thinly because the sweetness of the fondant layer may overshadow the flavor of the cake. Use a thin layer of buttercream under the fondant layer to adhere the paste to the cake.

1 Prepare the cupcake with a thin layer of buttercream, either piped neatly or spread over with a palette knife.

2 Roll out the fondant to your preferred thickness, ⅛–³⁄₁₆ in. (3–5 mm).

3 Cut out a circle of the fondant paste, using a round cutter large enough to cover the top of the cupcake.

4 Place the disk of paste on top of the cupcake and press lightly. Smooth the paste with a cake smoother or a pad of the paste to polish and smooth the cupcake top neatly.

Covering a cake with rolled fondant or marzipan

Rolled fondant is sweet frosting that can be kneaded from quite a hard block into a soft pliable sheet of paste to drape over the cake or cupcake and create a smooth, clean finish that is not possible to create with any other frosting.

The covering is placed over a cake after it has been covered thinly in a buttercream layer. This smooths out any indentations, but also helps to stick the fondant to the cake.

Fondant can be embossed, textured, crimped, and indented while it is still soft, but over a period of hours the paste will become firm on the outside but still soft under the surface. It is important to remember to wrap any unused paste in a plastic bag to stop it from drying out and crumbling away.

Marzipan is a paste that is made from almonds, sugar, and egg and is a delicious covering usually used on a fruit cake. It seals in the moisture and provides a smooth surface to then decorate the cake. Marzipan can be treated in the same way as fondant to cover a cake, but it is rolled out slightly thicker—around ½ in. (1 cm) thick.

1 Knead the paste until soft and pliable. Place on a work surface lightly dusted with confectioner's sugar and roll out with a rolling pin. Lift the paste up frequently on the rolling pin to ensure that it isn't sticking. Don't turn the paste over—keep the rolled surface uppermost—this will be the outer surface of your cake.

2 Continue rolling out the paste until you have a uniform thickness of around ⅛–¼ in. (3–6 mm). Lift the paste on the rolling pin and drape it over the cake. Use your hands to smooth the paste around the cake sides.

3 Use a knife to cut off the excess paste roughly first, then go around the cake again, trimming neatly to the base of the cake.

4 Use a cake smoother to create a neat, smooth finish to the sides and top of the cake.

5 Finish the cake covering by smoothing over with a pad of the paste—running it all over the cake will polish the paste and give a natural shine.

Flower Techniques

Making flowers in gum paste

Gum-paste flowers can be rolled very thinly, creating very realistic flowers for cupcakes and cakes. They can be wired or unwired and arranged in sprays or singly to make an ordinary cake into a talking point. There are dozens of cutters available to make every conceivable flower; however, this is a considerable expense. In this book some cutters have been used, but also templates that can be found at the back of the book (see pages 136–139). Try to buy or find a real flower to refer to when making a sugar flower—you will find it easier to make more realistic. If this isn't possible, look the flower up on the Internet. Follow the instructions for each individual flower in Chapter 2, but basic techniques are explained in detail on the following pages.

Mexican hat method for pulled flowers and cutter flowers

This technique is used for flowers such as stephanotis (see page 88) or jasmine (see page 55).

1 Take a small pinch of paste and roll it into a ball.

2 Start twisting the paste on the top while flattening the base.

Using modeling chocolate and marzipan

Modeling chocolate and marzipan need a little extra care when making flowers. The pastes are quite sticky and can become difficult to shape and mold if they become too warm from being worked. Unwired flowers are generally made from marzipan or chocolate—wiring with this sort of medium would be difficult because the paste has to be rolled more thickly than gum paste and the wire would not be able to support it easily. When coloring the pastes, work quickly then wrap in a plastic bag to allow the paste to cool and firm up again. The process of coloring will have made the paste warm and soft and started melting the oils within the paste.

1 Take a piece of white modeling chocolate and place between two sheets of plastic. A plastic sleeve, similar to one that notes can be filed in, is perfect; slit it down two sides, leaving one side attached. This makes it easier to get to the chocolate if necessary.

2 Roll out the paste between the two sheets of plastic—this will ensure that it will not stick to the work surface and the use of confectioner's sugar is not required.

3 Continue pulling the paste, thinning out the base.

4 Use a toothpick or Celstick to flatten the base further.

5 At this point, you can use a cutter to shape the base into the flower shape, use a template (see pages 136–139), or cut the shape freehand using an X-acto knife.

Wiring flowers for non-edible cakes

Gum-paste flowers can be wired or unwired. Unwired flowers need support while drying to give movement to the petals; wired flowers can be shaped and positioned to look as realistic as possible. The petals and leaves can be wired together, then taped using floral tape. The wires need to be wrapped in the tape not only to attach the petals to each other but also to hide them and create the stem of the flower. Floral tape is a crêpe-like paper that has been coated in wax; it is reversible and slightly stretchy, and sticks to itself as you apply it. The tape is available in a multitude of colors, including white—the most versatile, since you can use petal dust to color it. Green tape is excellent for stems and brown for branches and twigs.

Inserting wires into petals/leaves

1 There are many ways of inserting wires into petals and leaves, requiring various pieces of equipment. However there is a straightforward way to do this without any extra equipment. Wires come in different thicknesses, they are gauged—14-gauge (1.6 mm) wire being very thick and strong, and 33-gauge (0.2 mm) wire being very fine indeed. The choice of gauge depends on how much support the paste requires—large leaves will need a lot more support than a delicate orchid petal. Roll out the paste for the petal or leaf to a thickness of ⅛ in. (3 mm).

2 Cut out the shape with a cutter or template (see opposite).

3 Cut a short length of wire and insert it into the petal or leaf, running it up where the central vein of the shape would be. Press over the wire, taking care not to pierce the paste.

4 Take a Celstick or toothpick and roll the paste either side of the wire to a thickness of ¹⁄₃₂–¹⁄₁₆ in. (1–2 mm).

Cutting and veining flowers and leaves

There is a cutter and veiner for just about every conceivable flower or leaf you can imagine. The cost of purchasing cutters and veiners is enormous and not always necessary. Many petals and leaves can be cut freehand or with a template (see pages 136–139), as long as you don't have too many to cut. The time to buy a cutter is when you are sure you will use it frequently. Cutters for a rose, lily, and orchid are excellent examples to start with. Wipe the edges of the cutter after each use, as this removes any grains of sugar that might damage the edges of the next shape. Petals and leaves can also be veined by hand or by using a flower veiner. Alternatively, a general veiner can be obtained that will vein both sides of the petal or leaf at the same time—some will also shape the petal or leaf.

Veining petals or leaves

Place the petal or leaf on one side of the veiner, making sure that it is lined up straight, then place the top of the veiner over the paste and press firmly to vein both sides of the leaf or petal at the same time. Remove the shape carefully from the veiner.

Veining by hand

Use the flower veining tool to score the top of the petal or leaf with characteristic lines in keeping with whichever petal or leaf you are working on.

Using cutters

Place the cutter on rolled paste, press firmly, and remove the cutter. The shape will come away with the cutter.

Cutting freehand

Place the template on rolled paste. Hold lightly so as not to indent the paste, then use an X-acto knife to cut out the shape. Don't drag the knife.

For cutting out long sections, use a metal-bladed pizza cutter.

Frilling technique

Softening and frilling petals or leaves will give them their characteristic appearance—the carnation, for example, has a very frilly edge. It also allows you to soften and thin the edges of the petals and leaves so that they look more delicate and realistic.

1 Place the shape on a foam pad. Use a ball tool, bone tool, or toothpick to soften or frill the edge of the shape.

2 Work around the shape, thinning and texturing the petal or leaf.

Creating flower centers

Making non-edible wired stamens

The center of the flower is generally made separately to the petals, using paste, cotton stamens, or plastic stamens. If you are using a non-edible center, make sure you tell the recipient of the cake. Wired flowers are never eaten, as they contain the wires within the petals. Stamen centers can be store bought and a wide array is available; however, they can also be made using cotton thread and dusted with pollen powder—a granular food color available in different colors—to represent pollen.

1 Take hold of a cotton reel in one hand and wrap the cotton around two fingers of the other hand.

2 Insert a hooked wired into each end of the threads, twisting and securing. Cut the threads halfway between the two wires.

3 Tape the ends of the wires with floral tape, incorporating the folded threads to secure in place.

4 Dampen the ends of the threads and dust with pollen powder. Should colored stamens be required, dust them with an appropriate-colored petal dust.

Making edible flower centers

There are molds available for making various sizes of flower centers, with different stamen patterns to suit any flower.

Alternative methods

Alternatively, they can be handmade with the use of a few simple kitchen implements.

1 Roll the paste into a ball and flatten it. Place in the mold and press firmly. Turn the mold upside down and tap hard to release the paste without distorting the shape.

2 Place the center into the flower and secure with edible glue or a dot of royal icing.

1 If you don't have a mold available, use a sifter to texture by pressing several times, turning the sifter after each one.

2 Using the pointed end of the flower veining tool or a toothpick, prick the paste several times to create a textured surface.

Creating edible stamens from noodles

Edible stamens are made from gum paste or Chinese noodles. The following steps show how to make edible stamens from store cupboard noodles and pollen powder. Gum-paste stamens can also be made by rolling out gum paste and cutting thin strips. Once these are dry, dampen the tip with water, and dip into pollen powder. Alternatively, there are stamen molds on sale that make lifelike stamens. One method of attaching stamens is described here. Follow the cotton stamen instructions on the relevant flower but replace cotton stamens with edible noodle stamens instead.

1 Soak the noodles in hot water for an hour. If colored stamens are required, add food color to the water before soaking. Sugar can also be added to the water but this is optional Lay the noodles out flat on parchment paper until dry—this will take a couple of days. When completely dry, store in an airtight container ready for use.

2 Dampen the tip of the noodle and then dip it into the pollen powder.

3 The stamens can then be inserted into the center of a flower. It is best to do this while the petals or center of the flower are still soft.

Drying petals and leaves

Wired petals and leaves are supported with their wires in the position for drying, so actual support is not required, but a useful piece of equipment is a wired drying stand that allows you to stand the wired piece up or hang it upside down while it dries. Unwired flowers require support until dry. You can use foam or paper towels rolled into cylinders; alternatively, there are pieces of drying equipment that can be purchased.

Use rolled-up paper towel as a support system.

A drying stand in action.

Unwired flowers can also be placed in shaped formers, either commercially purchased for this purpose or made from aluminum foil shaped to support the flower.

Working with color

Coloring with petal dust

1 Load a paintbrush with petal dust from the pot. Don't tip the dust directly from the pot, as it may all drop out and be wasted.

2 Place the dust on a piece of paper towel and work the dust onto the brush.

3 Dust the intended spot on the petal or leaf with the loaded paintbrush, taking care not to get dust onto any other area.

4 Build up the color with further layers of dust, rather than adding too much dust at one time.

Making a colored paint

1 Using a paintbrush, place a small amount of dust in a palette.

2 Add a few drops of clear alcohol and mix with a paintbrush. You can use water, but it takes longer to dry and may soften the paste while it dries. Alcohol evaporates quickly, so vodka is the liquid of choice.

3 Apply to the petal or leaf using a paintbrush. If the paint starts to thicken, add more drops of clear alcohol.

4 Build up the color as you paint. You can apply both pale and dark colors to add detail and depth to petal or leaf.

Color mixing with paste color

Use paste color to color gum paste, buttercream, royal icing, and fondant, but not chocolate or marzipan.

1 Take a clean toothpick, dip the end into the paste food color, and add this color to your paste.

2 Knead the paste to blend the color evenly.

Color mixing with petal dust

Use petal dust to color chocolate, marzipan, and gum paste, but not buttercream or royal icing.

1 Use a palette knife to place the petal dust on the gum paste.

2 Knead the paste to blend the color evenly.

Using non-edible floral tape

Floral tape is available in a width of ½ in. (1 cm). It is quite difficult to get a neat finish with this width, so it is a good idea to slice the tape into three thinner tapes. Unreel a section around 4 in. (10 cm) long and use scissors to snip this into three 4 in. (10 cm) lengths.

1 Attach one end of the tape to the tip of the wire, then pull the tape slightly with one hand while holding the wire with the other.

2 Twist the wire while maintaining the tension on the tape, allowing the tape to cover the wire. Continue along the length of the wire.

Flower
Directory

A directory of 75 flowers organized into five different mediums. Perfect flowers to stand alone or be grouped together to make elegant decorations for celebration cakes.

Summer flowers

A pastel-themed summer garden
celebration cake, featuring lilac,
apple blossom, poppies, and
buttercups. The cake is finished with
a simple fringe of grass around the
base. Sprinkle loose petals across
the cake's surface.

Spring flowers

A spring-themed, two-tier cake,
decorated with chocolate flowers:
daffodils, hydrangea, primrose, and
lily of the valley. Strips of balls
in different colors and sizes
link the displays together.

Christmas flowers

Shaped like an ivy leaf and the board
decorated with snowballs and
nonpareils, this Christmas cake
features marzipan, ivy dusted around
the edges with gold, Christmas
roses, pine cones, a poinsettia, deep
red bows, stars, and gold baubles.
A perfect cake for Christmas Day.

Chocolate Flowers

Tools & Materials

- Basic chocolate tool kit, minus bone tool (see page 14)
- Ball tool
- Large 2 in. (5 cm) rose petal cutter or template (see page 136)

Makes one flower
- ⅞ oz (25 g) white modeling chocolate
- Pale orange petal dust

Rose

ADVANCED
01

The elegant rose is made of chocolate, a perfect medium to show off the intricacies of the flower.

1 Color the modeling chocolate with pale orange petal dust, and leave it to firm up.

2 Roll out the chocolate between the plastic sheets to a thickness of ⅛ in. (3 mm).

3 Using a cutter or template, cut out 10 rose petal shapes and place on a foam pad.

4 Use the ball tool to soften the edges, but don't press too hard—the chocolate is soft and you may make a hole.

5 Collect the remnants and shape into a cone. Insert the toothpick into the base.

6 Attach two petals to the cone using water and wrap around the cone neatly, overlapping one petal onto the other at one side and underlapping at the other side. Secure

at the base, but allow the petals at the top to open up slightly.

7 Attach three more petals, overlapping on one side and underlapping on the other as before, and curling the petals out.

8 Attach the remaining five petals in the same way, curling the petal tops out further to give a full rose appearance.

9 Leave to dry, then remove from the toothpick and place on your cake or cupcake.

3 4 4 5 6 7 8

Tools & Materials

- Basic chocolate tool kit (see page 14)
- Orchid cutting set or templates (see page 136)

Makes one flower
- 1 oz (30 g) white modeling chocolate
- Blue or purple petal dust
- Silver snowflake petal dust
- Buttercream or royal icing to secure the petals

INTERMEDIATE
02 Orchid

The orchid, elegant petals interestingly arranged; chocolate is the perfect medium to show this flower at its best.

1 Color the chocolate with the blue or purple petal dust and leave it to firm up. Roll out the chocolate between two plastic sheets to a thickness of 1⁄16–1⁄8 in. (2–3 mm), then cut out the petals using the cutters or templates: two large oval petals for the base of the flower, three smaller petals for the top section, and the central section.

2 Use the ball tool to soften the edges of the five petals.

3 Use the toothpick to frill the edges of the petals slightly.

4 Soften the central section of the flower with the bone tool, rubbing the tool over the whole shape, enlarging it slightly and also gently curling the parts of the shape inward.

5 Position the three smaller upper petals on the cake or cupcake and secure in place with a dot of buttercream or royal icing. Then position the two large oval petals underneath at either side of the center of the flower, using dots of buttercream or royal icing to secure.

6 Place the central section on the center of the flower, again securing with dots of buttercream or royal icing.

7 Take a pinch of chocolate and roll into a small teardrop shape that will fit inside the center of the flower. Indent down each side of the teardrop and attach the pointed end to the center of the flower.

8 When the flower is dry (two to four hours), dust it with the blue or purple petal dust and add silver snowflake petal dust for shimmer.

1   2   3   3   4   7

Tools & Materials

- Basic chocolate tool kit (see page 14)
- Lily cutters or template (see page 136)
- Lily petal veiner (optional)
- Cotton stamens x 6

Makes one flower
- 1 oz (30 g) white modeling chocolate
- Brown petal dust
- Orange petal dust
- Paper towel

Inedible stamens
For edible stamens, see page 29

Lily

The lily offers simple understated elegance.

1 Roll a pea-size chocolate ball into a sausage shape and insert a toothpick through the end to make the pistil.

2 Attach the stamens around the pistil and toothpick, using water and a tiny strip of modeling chocolate if necessary.

3 Dust the stamens and pistil with the brown petal dust. Leave to allow the chocolate pistil to firm up.

4 Color the remaining modeling chocolate with the orange petal dust and leave it to firm up.

5 Roll out the chocolate between the plastic sheets to a medium thickness of 1/16–1/8 in. (2–3 mm). Using the cutter or template, cut out three broad petals and three narrow petals.

6 Place on a foam pad and soften and thin the edges with the bone tool, taking care not to press too hard and tear the petal.

7 If using the veiner, press and vein each petal. If not, use the flower veining tool and draw the pointed end of the tool down the center of each petal, then do the same down either side of the central line.

8 Place the veined petals on the foam pad again and soften the edges, this time with the side of the toothpick, allowing the grain of the stick to texture the petals a little to add depth.

9 Attach the three broad petals first to the central stamen arrangement using water. Hold for a few seconds until secure, then set aside, supporting the petals in a curved-out position until firm.

10 Attach the narrower three petals in the same way, supporting them again until set.

11 When the flower is dry, pull out the toothpick and position the flower on your cake or cupcake.

12 Dust the petals with orange petal dust.

3   3   5   6   8

EASY

04 Peony

The peony comes in shades of bright pink, red, yellow, or white. They can have few petals to the bloom or many petals, giving a full, blowsy flower.

1 Roll out half of the modeling chocolate between the plastic sheets to a thickness of ⅛ in. (3 mm). Cut out three petal shapes 2 in. (5 cm) in size.

2 Place the petals on the foam pad and soften and enlarge the shapes using the ball tool.

3 Frill the petal edges using the bone tool, pressing fairly firmly; be sure not to overdo it, as the chocolate will tear.

4 Place each petal edge to the edge of the foam pad and frill the petal further with the toothpick.

5 Prepare all three shapes in the same way, then stack the petals on top of each other, offsetting them and securing in place with water. Curl the petals in slightly, and if necessary, hold in place with folded pieces of paper towel until firm.

6 Re-roll the remnants of chocolate to a thickness

of ¹⁄₃₂ in. (1 mm) and cut out two petal shapes.

7 Soften the edges, as in step 3.

8 Attach as before, curling the petals in further.

9 Color the rest of the chocolate with orange petal dust.

10 Pinch a pea-size amount of chocolate and roll into a ball, flatten, and prick the surface with the toothpick to make the center of the flower.

11 Roll the remaining chocolate into a short strip approximately 1 x ½ in. (25 x 12.5 mm). Score along the strip with the X-acto knife, cutting through one long side to make a fringe. Attach around the edge of the flattened ball and secure to the center of the petals.

12 Delicately dust the edges of the petals with pale pink petal dust.

Tools & Materials

- Basic chocolate tool kit (see page 14)
- Four-petal blossom cutter or template (see page 137)
- Paper towel

Makes three small flowers

- 1 oz (30 g) white modeling chocolate
- Orange petal dust
- Pale pink petal dust

2   3   4   5

10

11

Forget-Me-Not

Bright blue flowers with bright yellow centers, forget-me-nots are also found in shades of pink and white. A popular garden flower, perfect for a summer garden party cake.

1 Color two-thirds of the chocolate with the bright blue petal dust. Color half the remaining chocolate with the yellow petal dust. Leave the chocolate to firm up.

2 Roll out the blue chocolate between the plastic sheets to a thickness of ⅟₃₂ in. (1 mm).

3 Cut out as many blossoms as you desire— you could make them all the same size or use two cutters/templates and make two different sizes.

4 Place the flowers on the foam pad and, using the smaller end of the bone tool, soften the petal edges and curl them.

5 Indent the center of each flower with the pointed end of the flower veining tool.

6 Take a tiny pinch of yellow chocolate, roll into a ball, and secure in the center of the flower with water. Use the veining tool to indent the yellow center into the flower.

7 Arrange the flowers on the cake interspersing them with balls of white chocolate made from the remaining modeling chocolate.

Tools & Materials

- Basic chocolate tool kit (see page 14)
- Small five-petal blossom cutter

Makes 10 flowers and 10 balls
- ½ oz (15 g) white modeling chocolate
- Bright blue petal dust
- Yellow petal dust

3

4

6

7

Mimosa

The mimosa's leaves fold up on touch and its flowers are held in clusters.

Tools & Materials
- Basic chocolate tool kit (see page 14)
- Paper towel
- Leaf template (see page 136)

Makes three leaves and 16 balls
- 1 oz (30 g) white modeling chocolate
- Yellow pollen powder
- Yellow petal dust
- Green petal dust

1 Color half the chocolate with yellow petal dust and the other half with green. Leave the chocolate to firm up.

2 Roll the yellow chocolate into around 15 balls, of several sizes.

3 Brush the balls with water, then roll them in yellow pollen powder. Leave to dry.

4 Roll out the green chocolate between the plastic sheets to a thickness of 1/16 in. (2 mm), then cut out several elliptical shapes with the knife or use the template.

5 Place on the foam pad and soften and thin the edges using the bone tool, press lightly or you will tear the chocolate. Score down the center with the X-acto knife.

6 Frill the edges with the bone tool and score the leaves with the X-acto knife.

INTERMEDIATE

07 Tulip

Striking single-stemmed flowers in bright reds, pinks, yellows, and white, tulips look lovely with a simple chocolate bow (see page 71).

1 Color one-third of the chocolate with the orange petal dust, and one-third with the green petal dust, leaving the rest white. Leave the chocolate to firm up.

2 Shape a walnut-size ball of white chocolate into an egg shape, then insert a toothpick into the broad end and stand up in the foam pad to firm up.

3 Roll out the remaining white chocolate between the plastic sheets to a thickness of ¹⁄₁₆–⅛ in. (2–3 mm), then cut four petals using the rose petal cutter. Place on the foam pad.

4 Soften the chocolate and enlarge slightly using the ball tool. Work around the edge of the petal shapes, softening and thinning.

5 Draw the ball tool up each shape, curling the edges of two of the petals inward to give a slightly curved shape. Do the opposite on the other two petals, curving them outward slightly. Run the toothpick over these two petals to texture and grain them slightly.

6 Wrap two petals around the central shape, securing with water. Allow the petals to curve inward, and smooth the petals to the side with your fingers, making a neat and elegant shape.

7 Attach the final two petals in the same way using water, allowing them to curl out at the top. Smooth the petals down the sides and neaten underneath the shape, running the toothpick over the edges if necessary to continue the graining effect. Leave to firm up. Remove the toothpick.

8 There is enough chocolate here for two flowers, so follow the same procedure to make an orange tulip.

9 Roll a hazelnut-size ball of green chocolate into a sausage and thread onto a strand of dried spaghetti approximately 2 in. (5 cm) long, leaving ⅜ in. (1 cm) uncovered. Dampen the hole in the tulip base with a dot of water and insert the bare spaghetti until the green stem butts up against the tulip head.

10 Roll the remaining green chocolate between the plastic sheets and cut out five petal shapes to use as leaves.

11 Texture the leaves with the flower veining tool, drawing it up the center of the shape then at intervals to create leaf veins. Carefully attach to the stem of the tulip with water, holding them in place until they firm up or supporting them with the paper towel.

Tools & Materials

- Basic chocolate tool kit, minus bone tool (see page 14)
- Large rose petal cutter or template (see page 136)
- Dried spaghetti
- Paper towel

Makes two flowers
- 2½ oz (75 g) white modeling chocolate
- Orange petal dust
- Green petal dust

2   3   4   6   7   9   9   11

Tools & Materials
- Basic chocolate tool kit (see page 14)
- Ball tool
- Medium chrysanthemum flower cutter
- Paper towel
- Toothpick

Makes five to seven flowers
- 1 oz (30 g) white modeling chocolate
- Purple petal dust
- Yellow petal dust

EASY

08

Michaelmas Daisy

A simple bloom, elegantly presented against a pale buttercream backdrop.

1 Color three-quarters of the chocolate with purple petal dust and the remaining quarter with the yellow. Leave the chocolate to firm up.

2 Roll out the purple chocolate between the plastic sheets to a thickness of ¹⁄₁₆–⅛ in. (2–3 mm), and cut two shapes with the chrysanthemum cutter. Place on the foam pad.

3 Soften the shapes and thin slightly using the ball tool, then do the same with the bone tool, softening further and thinning more. Curl the petals up slightly too, drawing the tool from tip to center.

4 Attach one shape to the other, offsetting the petals between each other slightly and securing in place with water.

5 Shape a pinch of the yellow chocolate into a ball that fills the center of the flower—it should reach the base of the petals so that they look as if they are sprouting out of the yellow center.

6 Flatten the balls, dampen with water, and press into the yellow dust to give a "pollen" effect. Alternatively, prick over the whole of the center with the toothpick or the pointed end of the flower veining tool, or use a flower mold (see page 28) to texture.

7 Secure in the center of the flower using water.

8 Leave the petals to firm up in a slightly curved position—this is best achieved by rolling up the paper towel tightly to make a strip and coiling it around into a ring. Tuck this under the petals, with the center of the flower over the center of the ring, and allow the petals to firm up before moving.

Tools & Materials

- Basic chocolate tool kit (see page 14)
- Primrose flower cutter
- Small sauce bowl with saucer on top

Makes 10 flowers
- 1 oz (30 g) white modeling chocolate
- Yellow petal dust
- Orange petal dust
- Cocoa butter shavings

Primrose 09

INTERMEDIATE

The primrose is a colorful flower, found in woodland and around streams—a sign of spring.

1 Color the modeling chocolate with yellow petal dust, blend well, and then leave to firm.

2 Roll out the chocolate between the plastic sheets to a thickness of 1/16–1/8 in. (2–3 mm), then cut out the required number of flower shapes.

3 Place the flowers on the foam pad and soften with the bone tool, enlarging the flower slightly, then work the ends of each petal to thin and frill just a little.

4 Indent the center with the pointed end of the flower veining tool.

5 Shave a few curls of cocoa butter on the saucer and place over the small sauce bowl filled with boiling water to melt. Mix in a few grains of orange petal dust to make a paint.

6 Paint the center of the flowers with the paint.

1

3

6

INTERMEDIATE
10

Cala Lily

An elegant wedding flower, signifying purity and beauty.

1 Take a hazelnut-size pinch of white modeling chocolate, color with yellow petal dust, and roll it into a sausage shape. Push a toothpick through the sausage shape to make the central stamen.

2 Paint the stamen with water and cover with yellow pollen powder. Leave to firm up.

3 Color the remaining modeling chocolate with white petal dust, to make the chocolate a little whiter. Leave the chocolate to firm up.

4 Roll out the chocolate between the plastic sheets to a thickness of ⅛ in. (3 mm), then cut out the lily petal using a cutter or a template.

5 Place on the foam pad. Using the flower veining tool, soften and thin the edge of the petal, working all the way around. Take care not to press too firmly or you will tear the chocolate.

6 Curl the edges of the petal back with your fingers.

7 Wrap around the yellow stamen, securing in place with water. Allow the sides of the petal to overlap, further securing the petal in position, then open up the flower.

8 Dust the stem of the cala lily with the green petal dust to give the impression of the stem.

9 Dust the flower with the sparkle petal dust and support on rolled-up paper towel until firm.

10 When the flower is dry, carefully twist and pull the toothpick out, and then position the flower on the cake.

1   2   4   5

Tools & Materials

- Basic chocolate tool kit, minus flower veining tool (see page 14)
- Anthurium flower cutter or template (see page 137)
- Anthurium flower veiner
- Paper towel

Makes one flower
- 1 oz (30 g) white modeling chocolate
- Yellow petal dust
- Red petal dust
- Yellow pollen powder

Anthurium

EASY
11

A dramatic flower from the tropics, chocolate gives the perfect waxy appearance!

1 Color a pea-size ball of chocolate with yellow petal dust and the remainder with red petal dust. Leave the chocolate to firm up.

2 Roll out the red chocolate between the plastic sheets to a thickness of 1/16–1/8 in. (2–3 mm).

3 Cut out the anthurium shape with either a cutter or a template.

4 Place on the foam pad, running the bone tool around the edges to soften and thin the petal.

5 If you have an anthurium flower veiner, use it now—if not, use the bone tool, pressing the tool several times across the surface of the flower to give the distinctive appearance.

6 Roll up the paper towel tightly to make a strip and coil it around into a ring. Tuck this under the flower, with the center of the flower over the center of the ring, and leave the flower to firm up.

7 Roll the yellow chocolate into a sausage shape and insert a toothpick to assist in maintaining the shape.

8 Paint water over the stamen and roll it in yellow pollen powder.

9 Wrap the anthurium flower around the base of the stamen and support on the rolled-up paper towel until firm.

10 Carefully twist and pull the toothpick out, and then position the flower on the cake.

INTERMEDIATE

12 Anemone

A bold spring flower, the anemone appears in an array of colors and has a strong black center.

1 Color three-quarters of the modeling chocolate with the purple petal dust. Leave the chocolate to firm up.

2 Roll out the purple chocolate between the plastic sheets to a thickness of ⅛ in. (3 mm). Using a five-petal blossom cutter or a template, cut out two petal blossom shapes.

3 Place on the foam pad and soften the flower using the bone tool.

4 Run the bone tool around the edge of all the petals, thinning the edge and frilling slightly.

5 Place one flower on top of the other, offsetting the petals, and secure with water. Leave the petals to firm up in a curved position—roll up the paper towel tightly and coil it around into a ring. Tuck this under the petals, with the flower over the center of the ring.

6 Color the remaining chocolate with the black petal dust.

7 Roll the black chocolate out between the plastic sheets to a thickness of ¹⁄₁₆ in. (2 mm). Cut a strip approximately 1½ x ½ in. (3 x 1 cm).

8 Make little cuts down one side of the strip with the X-acto knife to make a fringe effect.

9 Using the black remnants, make a ball of chocolate, flatten, then prick with either a toothpick or a flower veining tool to texture.

10 Wrap the fringe around the black flower center, using water to secure. Position in the center of the flower, securing with water.

Tools & Materials

- Basic chocolate tool kit, minus bone tool (see page 14)
- Celstick
- Jasmine cutter
- General leaf cutter or template (see page 136)

Makes six flowers and three leaves
- 1 oz (30 g) white modeling chocolate
- Green petal dust
- Pink petal dust
- Silver snowflake petal dust

Jasmine   INTERMEDIATE 13

A fragrant flower that grows outside in southern Europe, and a perfect filler flower for cake arrangements.

1 Take two-thirds of the of modeling chocolate, divide into six equal portions, and roll and pinch each one up like a Mexican hat (see page 24), but pinched thinly.

2 Roll the flat part of the flower with the Celstick to thin, then thread the cutter over the raised center and cut out the flower.

3 Hold the flower in your hand and indent the center with the flower veining tool, then draw the tool up from the center to part way up each petal, indenting the flower as you go and making the center larger.

4 Leave the flower to dry upside down on the trumpet section. Repeat steps 2–4 to make five more flowers.

5 Color the remaining modeling chocolate with green petal dust and roll out to a thickness of 1/16 in. (2 mm) between the plastic sheets. Cut out two leaf shapes.

6 Use the pink petal dust to accentuate the center and base of the flower. Dust with silver snowflake petal dust.

7 Place the leaf shape on the foam pad, soften the edges using the ball tool, then score the leaf with the flower veining tool to texture. Dust with green petal dust to further naturalize the leaf, as seen in the image above.

EASY

14 Camellia

The camellia has glossy, dark green leaves and large flowers made up of intricately arranged petals. This one uses red petal dust, but you could make a camellia in white shading through the pinks to red.

1 Color ¼ oz (7 g) of the modeling chocolate with the green petal dust and the remainder with the red petal dust. Leave the chocolate to firm up.

2 Roll the red chocolate between the plastic sheets to a thickness of ¹⁄₁₆–⅛ in. (2–3 mm), then cut out one extra-large, two large, three medium, and three small five-petal shapes. Place them all on the foam pad.

3 Pinch together a pea-size amount of red chocolate to make a central ball for the center of the flower.

4 Soften each petal with the bone tool. Run the tool around the edge of the petals, thinning and slightly frilling.

5 Move each of the five petals in turn to the edge of the foam pad and, using the toothpick, soften the chocolate, allowing the stick to texture the petals slightly.

6 Curl the edges of the petals with the bone tool.

7 Work all the blossoms in the same way.

8 Take the three smallest blossoms, place the ball of chocolate in the center of one, and secure in place with water. Curl the petals around the ball, and sit it onto the second and third of the smallest petals, offsetting the petals and curling them up around the ball too to make the center of the camellia.

9 Continue with the medium, large, and extra-large blossom shapes, adding them in size order, offsetting the petals as you work.

10 Curl the petals slightly on the larger blossoms, to give a depth to the flower.

11 Roll out the green chocolate between the plastic sheets, cut out two leaves using the leaf cutter, and place on the foam pad.

12 Soften the edges of the leaves with the bone tool. Using the flower veining tool, draw the pointed end down each leaf shape to texture the central stem, following with the rest of the leaf, or, alternatively, use the leaf veiner. Dust with silver snowflake petal dust, if desired.

Tools & Materials

- Basic chocolate tool kit (see page 14)
- Five-petal blossom cutters (small, medium, large, and extra large)
- Rose leaf cutter
- Rose leaf veiner (optional)

Makes one flower and two leaves
- 1½ oz (45 g) white modeling chocolate
- Red petal dust
- Green petal dust
- Silver snowflake petal dust (optional)

1   3   4   5   6   12   12

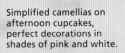

Simplified camellias on
afternoon cupcakes,
perfect decorations in
shades of pink and white.

ADVANCED

15 Bindweed

Bindweed modeled in subtle shades of pink. There is a striped version of this flower, morning glory, that's also fun to make.

1 Color the chocolate with the white petal dust. Leave the chocolate to firm up.

2 Pinch out a hazelnut-size piece of chocolate and roll into a ball, making it smooth and shiny. Then pinch one side of the ball, to make a Mexican hat shape (see page 24).

3 Flatten the brim of the Mexican hat section. Use the side of the Celstick to roll this flat, working all the way around.

4 Thread the circle cutter over the raised center, and cut out a circle again.

5 Continue thinning out the flat area with a Celstick, and cut off the excess again.

6 Turn the flower over and holding it in your hand, use the flower veining tool to indent the center, then use the Celstick to thin the flower out to make it look like the inside of a trumpet—or use a

toothpick if you prefer. Work quickly, as the chocolate will melt.

7 Curl back the edge of the trumpet. Then turn the flower upside down on the trumpet section and leave to firm up. This will further curl the edge of the flower.

8 Take five to seven stamens and attach to a toothpick with a half pea-size ball of modeling chocolate.

9 Dust the stamens with white pollen powder.

10 Push the toothpick through the center of the trumpet and out through the point, pinching the chocolate around the stamens.

11 Stand the flower up and support it if necessary and leave to firm up.

12 Stand the saucer over the sauce bowl with boiling water, shave a few

curls of cocoa butter onto the saucer, and add enough pink petal dust to make the desired shade. Paint the edges of the flower, as shown above.

13 Dust the center of the flower with the yellow petal dust. When dry, after 24 hours, pull out the toothpick before placing the flower on the cake surface.

3   6   10

Tools & Materials

- Basic chocolate tool kit (see page 14)
- Celstick
- Periwinkle flower cutter
- Periwinkle leaf cutter
- 5 stamens (small white cotton)

Makes three flowers and three leaves
- 1 oz (30 g) white modeling chocolate
- Pale lilac petal dust
- Green petal dust
- Yellow pollen powder

Inedible stamens
For edible stamens, see page 29

Periwinkle   INTERMEDIATE 16

The periwinkle has striking stellar-blue flowers, a color that can be recreated with pale lilac petal dust.

1 Color all but ⅛ oz (3.5 g) of the chocolate with the pale lilac petal dust. Color the remaining chocolate green for the leaf. Leave to firm up.

2 Take a hazelnut-size pinch of the chocolate and roll into a smooth ball. Then pinch one side of the ball, twisting and pulling to make a Mexican hat shape (see page 24).

3 Flatten the brim of the Mexican hat section. Use the side of the Celstick to roll this flat, working all the way around.

4 Thread the periwinkle cutter over the pulled-up section in the center and cut out a periwinkle shape.

5 Continue thinning out the flat area with a Celstick or toothpick. Run the toothpick over the petals to thin them slightly and to texture them. Cut off the excess again.

6 Turn the flower over. Holding it in your hand, use the flower veining tool to indent the center, then use the Celstick to thin out the petals to make it look like the inside of a trumpet. Work quickly, as the chocolate will melt.

7 Curl back the edge of the trumpet. Then turn the flower upside down on the trumpet section and leave it to firm up. This will further curl the edge of the flower.

8 Take five stamens and attach to a toothpick with a half pea-size ball of modeling chocolate.

9 Dust the stamens with pollen powder.

10 Push the toothpick through the center of the trumpet and out through the point, pinching the chocolate to the stamens.

11 Stand the flower up and support it if necessary. Leave to firm up.

12 Dust the flower with lilac petal dust to accentuate the color and give depth to the coloring. When dry, after 24 hours, pull out the toothpick.

13 Roll out the green chocolate between the plastic sheets to a thickness of ¹⁄₁₆–⅛ in. (2–3 mm). Cut out the leaf, using the cutter. Place the leaf on the foam pad, and texture with the flower veining tool.

2   4   10   13   13

ADVANCED

17 # Water Lily

This is a striking flower that lasts only a few days, quickly replaced with a new flower—and there are so many colors to choose from!

1 Color three-quarters of the chocolate with the pink petal dust. Split the remaining chocolate in half and color half yellow and half green using the petal dusts. Leave to firm up. Roll the pink chocolate between the plastic sheets to a thickness of ⅛ in. (3 mm). Cut out 12 petal shapes in total. Cut off the base of the petal to give a flattened end. Place on the foam pad. Soften the edges of the petals with the ball tool.

2 Using the pointed end of the flower veining tool, vein each petal of the blossom, press firmly up the center, and pull the chocolate a little to shape the petal into an oval. Pinch the point of the petal slightly to exaggerate the shape.

3 Curl the petal up with the bone tool, then place on rolled-up paper towel to maintain the shape of the petals while they firm up. Do the same with the second and subsequent petal shapes.

4 Place one petal on top of another, offsetting the petals in rows, securing with water and pressing gently together. Support with rolled paper towel until the petals are holding themselves; this will take approximately two or three hours.

5 Take half the yellow chocolate. Roll into a ball, flatten, and prick several times with the toothpick to make the center of the flower. Dust with pollen powder if desired.

6 Roll the remaining yellow chocolate into a strip approximately 1 x ½ in. (25 x 12.5 mm). Score along one long side of the strip with the X-acto knife to make a fringe. Attach around the edge of the flattened ball and secure to the center of the flower with water.

7 Roll out the green chocolate between plastic sheets to a thickness of ⅛ in. (3 mm). Cut out a circle shape with a circle cutter or freehand. Use the flower veining tool to indent the circle edge, as in the image.

8 Use the same tool to texture the leaf with veins.

Tools & Materials

- Basic chocolate tool kit (see page 14)
- Rose petal cutter, 1–1¼ in. (2.5–3 cm) or template (see page 136)
- Paper towel
- Circle cutter (optional)

Makes one flower and one leaf
- 1 oz (30 g) white modeling chocolate
- Pink petal dust
- Yellow petal dust
- Green petal dust
- Yellow pollen powder (optional)

1   2   5   6   6   7   8

Striking water lilies show their elegant petals.

EASY
18 Ivy Wreath

Ivy leaves are the perfect "filler" leaf for many flower arrangements. Here they are shown in a seasonal wreath.

1 Color ¼ oz (7 g) of the chocolate green and ⅔ oz (14 g) red. Color the rest of the chocolate yellow.

2 Roll the green chocolate out between the plastic sheets to a thickness of ¹⁄₁₆–⅛ in. (2–3 mm).

3 Cut out the leaves either with a cutter or a template, then place them on the foam pad.

4 Soften the edges with the bone tool.

5 Place the leaf on the leaf veiner and emboss the surface to make it

look more realistic. If you don't have an ivy leaf veiner, use the pointed end of the flower veining tool to vein the leaves by hand.

6 Make the little flowers from red and yellow chocolate by following the forget-me-not instructions on page 46.

Make as many berries from red chocolate as desired.

7 Position the leaves onto the cake or cupcake along with the flowers and berries, and secure in place with water.

Tools & Materials

- Basic chocolate tool kit (see page 14)
- Ivy leaf cutter or template (see page 137)
- Ivy leaf veiner

Makes eight leaves, 20 flowers, and 20 berries
- 1 oz (30 g) white modeling chocolate
- Green petal dust
- Red petal dust
- Yellow petal dust

For the flower, see the forget-me-not on page 46.

3

5

6

6

6

6

Pansy

They come in so many different shades, make one in your favorite color!

Tools & Materials

- Basic chocolate tool kit, minus flower veining tool (see page 14)
- Pansy blossom flower cutter or templates (see page 139)
- Paper towel
- Small sauce bowl with saucer on top

Makes three flowers
- 1 oz (30 g) white modeling chocolate
- Lilac petal dust
- Yellow petal dust
- Cocoa butter shavings

1 Take a hazelnut-size ball of modeling chocolate and color with the lilac petal dust. Reserve the same amount of white chocolate for the center of the pansy. Roll the remaining white chocolate and the lilac chocolate between the plastic sheets to a thickness of 1/16–1/8 in. (2–3 mm).

2 Cut out three small petals (one petal from the lilac chocolate and two from the white

chocolate) and one large petal from the white chocolate. Place them on the foam pad.

3 Soften the edges with the bone tool, but don't press too firmly as the chocolate will tear.

4 Frill the large white petal and the lilac petal more than the other two petals.

5 Position the petals in order: the lilac petal at the back, then the two

small white ones either side with their centers lined up with the lilac center, and the largest petal on top, as per the image. Secure with water.

6 Leave to firm up on a rolled-up paper towel. Take the remnant of white modeling chocolate, color it yellow with the petal dust, and roll it into a ball. Position in the center of the pansy and indent with the flower veining tool.

7 Place shavings of cocoa butter on the saucer, then place over the small sauce bowl with boiling water, to allow it to melt.

8 Make purple and yellow paints with the melted cocoa butter and petal dusts. Following the colors in the photo, paint the petals of the pansy.

2   3   3   3   6

Marzipan
Flowers

Rose

This is the easiest rose to make; by wrapping the paste around itself, the stylized flower appears.

Tools & Materials

- Basic marzipan tool kit (see page 14)
- Pizza cutter
- Textured rolling pin (optional)

Makes one large and five small flowers, and 12 balls
- 1 oz (30 g) natural-colored marzipan
- Red petal dust

1 Color the marzipan with the red petal dust, and leave the marzipan to firm up.

2 Roll the marzipan out between the plastic sheets to a thickness of $\frac{1}{16}$–$\frac{1}{8}$ in. (2–3 mm). It is not easy to manipulate the paste if it is too thin.

3 Cut the marzipan into rectangular strips approximately 1 x 4 in. (2.5 x 10 cm).

4 Texture the strip using the textured rolling pin, if desired.

5 Fold the strip gently in half along its length.

6 Roll the strip up, coiling it up quite tightly to start with to get a good center to the rose, then allow the coiling to become looser as you go along, creating the outer petals of the flower.

7 If you want smaller flowers, stop coiling at the desired point and cut away the excess marzipan.

4

6

INTERMEDIATE
21 Lily

This is a flower that needs some support while drying, as it is unwired. It is a perfect flower for a birthday cake.

1 Color the marzipan with the yellow petal dust, and then leave the marzipan to firm up.

2 Roll the marzipan between the plastic sheets to a thickness of $\frac{1}{16}$–$\frac{1}{8}$ in. (2–3 mm), then cut out three broad and three narrow petals using the cutters or templates. Place each petal on the foam pad.

3 Use the bone tool to soften around the edges of each petal, then use the lily petal veiner to texture the petals. If you do not have a petal veiner available, use the flower veining tool instead.

4 Curl the petals and support with rolled-up pieces of paper towel. Leave to firm up until the petals hold their own shape.

5 Attach the cotton stamens loosely to the toothpick with floral tape; alternatively, use a tiny strip of marzipan to secure the stamens in place. Wrap the floral tape tightly around the toothpick below the stamens, as you will be removing this later.

6 Dust the stamens with pollen powder to give the pollen effect.

7 Secure the petals around the stamen center with water. Attach the broad petals first, then the narrow ones.

8 Leave the flower to dry and set, supported on rolled-up paper towel, for approximately 48 hours.

Twist the toothpick while carefully holding the flower, removing the toothpick and floral tape, but leaving the stamens in place.

Tools & Materials

- Basic marzipan tool kit (see page 14)
- Lily petal cutter or template (see page 136)
- Lily petal veiner
- Cotton stamens (six or seven per flower)
- Floral tape
- Rolled-up paper towel

Makes one flower
- 1½ oz (45 g) natural-colored marzipan
- Yellow petal dust
- Yellow pollen powder

Inedible stamens
For edible stamens, see page 29

1   2   5   6   7

Lily (instructions
opposite) and coiled
fantasy flower
in gum paste
(see page 100).

ADVANCED

22 Orchid

The orchid is a delicate flower, so try to roll the paste as thinly as you can and support the petals while drying. The marzipan will hold its shape if it is dried for long enough.

1 Color three-quarters of the marzipan with pink petal dust. Leave to firm.

2 Roll the pink marzipan between the plastic sheets to a thickness of 1/16 in. (2 mm), and cut out three narrow petals, two larger petals, and the central section. Place on the foam pad.

3 Soften the edges of the five petals using the bone tool.

4 Frill the edges of the petals with the toothpick.

5 Soften the central part of the petals with the bone tool. Rub the tool over the whole shape, enlarging it slightly and gently curling the parts of the shape inward.

6 Using the ball tool, curl the central throat of the orchid, curl the two side elements inward and the lower bulbous section upward.

7 Use the orchid veiner to add texture to each of the petals. Support the petals with rolled-up paper towel.

8 Position the three smaller petals on the cake or cupcake as shown above and secure with a dot of royal icing. Position the two large semicircular petals on top, at either side of the center of the flower, securing as before.

9 Position the curled-up orchid throat on the center of the flower, again securing as before. Shade the petals with pink and red petal dust.

10 Take a pinch of pink marzipan and roll it into a small teardrop that will fit inside the center of the flower. Indent down each side of the teardrop and attach to the center of the flower by the pointed end.

11 Color the remaining marzipan with green petal dust. Allow the paste to firm up again. Roll out between the plastic sheets to a thickness of 1/8 in. (3 mm). Cut out a rough oval shape, texture with the flower veining tool, and attach behind the flower. Support with a rolled-up paper towel until firm, for approximately two or three hours.

2   2   2   3   3   4   6   10   10   11

Tools & Materials
- Basic marzipan tool kit (see page 14)
- Poinsettia cutters or templates (see page 139)
- Flower veining tool
- Rolled-up paper towel

Makes one flower
- 1 oz (30 g) natural-colored marzipan
- Red petal dust

Poinsettia ^{EASY}

EASY
23

The poinsettia's striking scarlet leaves, here made in marzipan, are perfect for decorating Christmas cakes.

1 Color two-thirds of marzipan red and the remaining third pink. Blend until even, and leave to firm up.

2 Roll out the red marzipan between the plastic sheets to a thickness of $1/16$–$1/8$ in. (2–3 mm).

3 Cut out the poinsettia bracts using the cutters or templates and an X-acto knife. Several sizes of bract are required, from very small up to large and four or five of each. Place on the foam pad.

4 Soften the edges of the bracts with the bone tool.

5 Run the flower veining tool up the center of the bracts to texture—you could use a poinsettia veiner, if available.

6 Attach the bracts in rosettes to the top of the cake or cupcake, using dots of water—start with the large bracts around the outside, working inward, overlaying the bracts with smaller ones.

7 Finish with tiny pink balls of marzipan in the center, using water to secure in place.

EASY
24 Holly and Berries

Another perfect decoration for a Christmas cake, easy to make, and effective when teamed up with the poinsettia and mistletoe.

1 Color a hazelnut-size ball of the marzipan with red petal dust, blend until even, and leave to firm up. Color the remaining marzipan with the green petal dust.

2 Roll the green marzipan out between the plastic sheets to a thickness of 1/16–1/8 in. (2–3 mm), then cut out seven to nine leaf shapes using either the cutter or a template.

3 Place on the foam pad and soften around the edges with the bone tool.

4 Use the holly leaf veiner to texture the leaf, or use the flower veining tool if you don't have a holly leaf veiner available.

5 Position the leaves on the cake or cupcake and secure with water.

6 Roll the red paste into small balls for the berries—three for the base of each leaf—and secure in the same way.

Tools & Materials

- Basic marzipan tool kit (see page 14)
- Holly leaf cutter or template (see page 139)
- Holly leaf veiner (optional)

Makes seven leaves and 24 berries
- 1 oz (30 g) natural-colored marzipan
- Red petal dust
- Green petal dust

2

4

6

Mistletoe

Easy to make and teams well with the other flowers used to decorate Christmas cakes.

Tools & Materials

- Basic marzipan tool kit (see page 14)
- General leaf cutter or template (see page 136)
- General leaf veiner

Makes seven leaves, 12–15 berries, and one bow
- 1½ oz (45 g) natural-colored marzipan
- White petal dust (or confectioner's sugar)
- Green petal dust
- Red petal dust

1 Color ¾ oz (21 g) of the marzipan with the green petal dust, ½ oz (14 g) of the marzipan with the white petal dust or confectioner's sugar, and ¼ oz (7 g) with the red petal dust. Leave to firm up.

2 Roll the green marzipan between the plastic sheets to a thickness of ⅛ in. (3 mm), then cut out seven leaves. Place on the foam pad.

3 Use the bone tool to soften around the edges of the leaves, elongating them. Using the flower veining tool or general leaf veiner, vein each leaf.

4 Position the leaves on the cupcake or cake and secure with water.

5 Shape the white marzipan into 12–15 balls for the berries of the mistletoe and attach in the same way.

6 Roll the red marzipan between plastic sheets to a thickness of ⅟₁₆–⅛ in. (2–3 mm). Cut two rectangular strips approximately ⅜ x 2¼ in. (1 x 6 cm). Cut one strip into two pieces, and cut a triangle out of one end of each piece for the ribbon ends. Fold the other rectangle centrally to form the bow.

7 Position the bow on the cake, with the two ribbon tails underneath, and secure in place with water. Use the remnants of red marzipan paste to make the center of the bow: roll out the paste as before, cutting a shorter rectangle but still ⅜ in. (1 cm) in width. Secure over the center of the bow with water.

2   3   5   6
6

EASY
26 # Bramble

This is a favorite of mine. The flowers here are made of gum paste, as natural marzipan is a yellow color, and I wanted a flower with a white base.

1 Color two-thirds of the marzipan with the purple petal dust, and leave to firm up. Color the remaining marzipan with the green petal dust.

2 Shape a hazelnut-size ball of the purple marzipan into a cone shape, then insert a toothpick through the flat base. You need one of these per bramble.

3 Make the remaining purple marzipan into tiny balls, attaching them to the cone with water. Press them together, working from the top to the base.

4 Roll the green marzipan between the plastic sheets to a thickness of 1/16–1/8 in. (2–3 mm), then cut out three to five leaves for each cupcake.

5 Place the leaves on the foam pad and soften around the edges with the bone tool.

6 Texture the leaves with the veiner or use the flower veining tool to vein by hand.

7 Remove the toothpick from the base of the bramble and attach it to the cake or cupcake with water.

8 The flower is made from gum paste. Follow the instructions for the cherry blossom (see page 106) but use yellow pollen powder for the pollen.

Tools & Materials

- Basic marzipan tool kit (see page 14)
- Rose leaf cutter or template (see page 136)
- Rose leaf veiner

Makes two berries and five leaves
- 1½ oz (45 g) natural-colored marzipan
- Purple petal dust
- Green petal dust
- Yellow pollen powder

For the flower, see page 106

Inedible stamens
For edible stamens, see page 29

These pretty bramble cupcakes would be perfect for a fall tea party.

27 Pinecone

This is easy if you have a mold and a little more challenging if you are making the pinecone freehand.

1 Color all of the marzipan with the brown petal dust, blend until even, and leave to firm up. Take a hazelnut-size piece and press it firmly into the mold. Scrape off any excess paste from the top, making the paste flush with the top of the mold.

2 Turn the mold over and tap until the shaped marzipan drops out cleanly. Make more pinecones using the same method.

3 If you don't have a mold available, shape the marzipan into an oval, then snip the side of the oval at regular intervals

with a pair of scissors to create a spiked effect.

4 Shape the remnants of marzipan into a sausage shape, approximately 1 x ¼ in. (2.5 x 0.5 cm) to represent the stalk of the pinecones.

Tools & Materials
- Pinecone mold
- Scissors (optional)

Makes three cones
- 1½ oz (45 g) natural-colored marzipan
- Brown petal dust

Hellebore

Hellebores are lovely, subtle flowers. Make them in a range of colors—greens, purples, pinks, and natural cream.

Tools & Materials

- Basic marzipan tool kit (see page 14)
- Large five-petal blossom cutter or template (see page 137)
- Cotton stamens (15 per flower)

Makes three flowers
- 1 oz (30 g) natural-colored marzipan
- Purple petal dust
- Yellow petal dust
- Yellow pollen powder (optional)

Inedible stamens
For edible stamens, see page 29

1 Color two-thirds of the marzipan with purple petal dust, blend until even, and leave to firm up.

2 Roll the marzipan out between the plastic sheets to a thickness of $\frac{1}{16}$–$\frac{1}{8}$ in. (2–3 mm).

3 Cut out the blossom and place on the foam pad.

4 Soften the edges of the petals with the bone tool, but don't press too firmly, otherwise you will tear the paste. Curl the edges inward, to a slight point.

5 Draw the bone tool from the edge of the petal to the center, to curl the paste upward and inward.

6 Color the remaining marzipan with the yellow petal dust. Roll into a ball, flatten, and texture with the toothpick to represent the center of the flower.

7 Dust the stamens with yellow pollen powder and insert them around the sides of the flower center.

8 Secure the flower center to the petal using water.

Gum Paste Flowers

Tools & Materials

- Basic gum paste tool kit (see page 14)
- 24-gauge (0.5 mm) wire
- Singapore orchid cutter kit
- Bone tool
- Floral tape (Nile green)
- Rolled-up paper towel
- Posy pick

Makes one flower
- 1 oz (30 g) gum paste
- Pink petal dust
- Green petal dust
- Silver snowflake petal dust

Inedible flower

Singapore Orchid

ADVANCED

29

The Singapore orchid is a delicate, elegant flower—not the easiest to make, but well worth the effort. The beautiful shading on the petals gives it a very realistic appearance.

1 Shape the column of the flower using the mold provided in the cutter kit. Insert a 24-gauge (0.5 mm) wire up the center of the column, then leave to dry.

2 Roll out a small amount of paste and cut out the broad throat petal using the cutter. Press the shape into the cutter as you cut to texture the paste.

3 Tap the shape out of the cutter, insert a 24-gauge. (0.5 mm) wire up the center, place on the foam pad, and soften the edges slightly with the bone tool.

4 Dampen the base of the petal and wrap it around the column, with the column facing in toward the petal. Tape the wires together using floral tape.

5 When dry, cut out, texture, and soften the triple petal shape and two single petals in the same way.

6 Place the two single petals on top of the triple petal shape, as shown below, and secure in place with a dot of water.

7 Take the throat section and place the base

against the point where the petals meet. Dampen with water, then pinch the petals around the base of the throat. Allow the lower section of the triple petal to stick out behind, then pinch it together.

8 Place on the foam pad, using a rolled-up paper towel to support it.

9 Dust the petals with the pink and green petal dust, then finish with a dusting of silver snowflake petal dust. Insert the posy pick into the cake, then insert the flower into this.

1   3   3   4   5   6

ADVANCED

30 Rose

The rose is the typical English flower that can be found in almost any color—the flower of weddings, birthdays, and afternoon tea. Looking at it, you can almost smell its aroma!

1 Color two-thirds of the paste with pink paste color. Take a hazelnut-size pinch of pink paste, shape into a cone, and push onto the end of a toothpick.

2 Roll out the remaining pink paste to a thickness of 1/32 in. (1 mm) and cut out five petals.

3 Place the petals on the foam pad and soften around the edges of two petals with the bone tool—rub the whole petal with the tool to soften the rest of the petal.

4 Take the toothpick and run it lightly around the edge of the petals.

5 Dampen the cone and wrap the two petals around the cone, overlapping on both sides.

6 Prepare the other three petals in the same way and attach to the cone, interlocking each petal with the previous to give a coil effect to the center of the flower. Curl the edges of the petals more using the toothpick to make them more frilly.

7 Continue preparing petals—five are required for the next row and seven for the row after—interlocking the petals as you attach them to the flower.

8 Leave the flower to dry for five minutes after you have added each row of petals—this makes it easier, as the previous row won't move about. It is a good idea to make several flowers at once, so by the time you get back to the first, it is dry enough to work on.

9 For the leaf, color the remaining paste with green paste color. Cut out the general leaf shape and vein using the general leaf veiner.

10 Dust the flower with pink petal dust, adding more at the center, then finish with a dust of silver snowflake petal dust. Dust the leaves with the green petal dust.

11 Before displaying the flower, pull out the toothpick from the base. Position on the cake.

Tools & Materials

- Basic gum paste tool kit, minus flower veining tool (see page 14)
- Rose petal cutter
- General leaf cutter or bramble leaf template (see page 138)
- General leaf veiner
- Bone tool
- Toothpick

Makes one large flower
- 1 oz (30 g) gum paste
- Pink paste color
- Green paste color
- Pink petal dust
- Silver snowflake petal dust
- Green petal dust

1   2   3   4   4   5   6   7   9   9   9   10

You could add one or more roses to your cakes or cupcakes, either with or without leaves, depending on your design requirements.

Tools & Materials

- Basic gum paste tool kit (see page 14)
- Lily cutter or template (see page 136)
- Lily petal and leaf veiner
- Bone tool
- Toothpick
- 24-gauge (0.5 mm) wire cut into thirds
- 8 cotton stamens
- Floral tape (green)
- Posy pick

Makes one flower and three leaves
- 1 oz (30 g) gum paste
- Yellow paste color
- Green paste color
- Brown pollen powder
- Red petal dust
- Pink petal dust
- Silver snowflake petal dust

Inedible flower

INTERMEDIATE

31

Starburst Lily

A very startling flower with a strong scent, the starburst lily is a definite statement flower.

1 Color a pea-size pinch of paste with yellow paste color, and shape it into a cone. Push in a small length of 24-gauge (0.5 mm) wire from the pointed end of the cone, leaving the other end flat for the stigma.

2 Brush eight stamens with water, and dust with brown pollen powder, then attach to the stigma with green floral tape. Tweak the stamens into a neat position.

3 Roll out two-thirds of the white gum paste to a thickness of 1/32–1/16 in. (1–2 mm). Cut out three small and three large petals, using the cutters or templates and an X-acto knife.

4 Thread a strand of 24-gauge (0.5 mm) wire through the base and three-quarters of the way up each petal. Place on the foam pad.

5 Soften around the edges of the petals, running the bone tool along the edge, thinning the paste.

Texture the petals by pressing between the lily veiner, then ruffle the edges of each petal with the bone tool.

6 Bend each petal into a natural position, pinch the base of the petal together to thin, and leave upright to dry for 20 minutes, either in a petal stand or in a wine glass. Repeat for all petals.

7 Dust the petals with red petal dust, drawing it up the petals from base to tip with the paintbrush, tailing off toward the tip.

Use the pink petal dust either side of the red, to blend out the color.

8 Tape the petals together, starting with the larger petals first, then place the smaller ones between and behind each large one.

9 Color the remaining paste with the green paste color, then roll out between plastic sheets to a thickness of 1/32–1/16 in. (1–2 mm). Cut out the three leaves using the smaller of the lily petal cutters or templates.

10 Insert a strand of 24-gauge. (0.5 mm) wire into the leaves, as for the petals.

11 Soften the edges of the leaves with the bone tool. Texture the leaf using the flower veining tool.

12 Use strands of floral tape to wire the leaves behind the flower head. Dust with silver snowflake petal dust if desired. Insert the posy pick into the cake, then insert the flower into this.

1 1 2 2 2 4 5 8 5 8 8 10 11

Tools & Materials

- Basic gum paste tool kit (see page 14)
- Large five-petal daisy cutter
- Small six-petal daisy cutter
- Bone tool
- Celstick
- Toothpick (optional)

Makes six flowers
- 1 oz (30 g) gum paste
- Yellow pollen powder
- Green paste color
- Green petal dust
- Silver snowflake petal dust (optional)

Star of Bethlehem

EASY

32

This flower is found on stalks of 10 or 15 flowers in nature, but they are so pretty and fresh, they look perfect displayed in a small group or individually on a cupcake.

1 Roll out two-thirds of the white gum paste to a thickness of ¹⁄₃₂–¹⁄₁₆ in. (1–2 mm). Cut out a large five-petal daisy shape and place on the foam pad.

2 Soften around the edges of the daisy with the bone tool, then use the Celstick to broaden and lengthen the petals, leaving a little texture as you work. If you prefer, you can do this with a toothpick.

3 Cut out a small six-petal daisy and work in the same way.

4 Draw the bone tool up each petal, curling them up together.

5 Dampen each point of the small daisy shape with a dot of water, then turn upside down into the pollen powder, allowing it to stick to the ends of each petal.

6 Position the smaller daisy in the center of the large daisy, securing it with a dot of water.

7 Take the remaining paste and color it with green paste color.

8 Take a pinch of paste and roll it into a ball. Flatten slightly, then using the X-acto knife, cut little triangles out of the ball.

9 Indent the cuts with the pointed end of the flower veining tool to neaten.

10 Position the green ball shape in the center of the flower and secure with a dot of water.

11 Dust with silver snowflake petal dust if desired.

ADVANCED

33 # Fuchsia

Fuchsias can be made in a multitude of different colors, dangling from thin stems, almost looking as though a gust of wind would blow the delicate flowers off.

1 Cut 4 in. (10 cm) of white floral tape, then cut into three strips lengthwise. Take five to seven stamens and attach to a 24-gauge (0.5 mm) wire, using the floral tape. Make sure the stamens are at different lengths, with one that stands out as the longest.

2 Paint the stamens using the red dusting powder. Allow to dry, then dust with the red petal dust. Blow off any excess.

3 Roll out a small pinch of white paste to a thickness of 1/32 in. (1 mm), cut out one blossom, and place on the foam pad.

4 Soften the edges of the petals with the ball tool, then using the toothpick or ball tool, frill the edges lightly. Draw the ball tool up the petals, curling them inward slightly.

5 Thread the blossom down the stamen stalk, molding and overlapping the petals around the stamens, securing the petals in place with a dot of water.

6 Allow to dry in an upturned position, so that the petals stay curled around the stamens.

7 Color 1/4 oz (7 g) paste with the red paste color to create a light pink color. Blend in the color.

8 Roll the paste into a ball, then create the sepal using the Mexican hat method (see page 24).

9 Cut out a base for the fuchsia using the X-acto knife. It requires four sepals, so cut one at each side, like a compass.

10 Soften the edges of the cut sepals with the ball tool on the foam pad, then use the ball tool to draw up each sepal—this will curl them back.

11 Thread the pink sepal down the stamen stalk behind the white blossom, and secure with a dot of water.

12 Color 1/2 oz (15 g) of paste with the green paste color. Thread a pea-size ball of green paste down the stamen, and secure it in place with a dot of water. Shape the ball so that it is slightly elongated and tapers onto the wire.

13 Tape the wire with thin strips of green floral tape. Dust the green paste and the tape where they join with green dusting powder.

14 Roll out 1/3 oz (10 g) green paste to make the leaves. Cut out the leaves using the leaf cutter or template and an X-acto knife.

15 Insert a strand of 24-gauge (0.5 mm) wire up the center of the leaf, then place it in the leaf veiner and press firmly. If you don't have a veiner, use the flower veining tool to create the veins by hand.

16 Tape the wire with green floral tape, then dust the wire and leaf with green petal dust to give a natural appearance. Attach the leaf to the flower using floral tape.

17 Make one more flower and two more leaves in the same way. Dust the whole display with silver snowflake petal dust if desired.

18 Insert the end of each stem into a posy pick; each posy pick will accommodate three stems.

Tools & Materials

- Basic gum paste tool kit (see page 14)
- Floral tape (white and green)
- Five to seven cotton stamens per flower
- 24-gauge (0.5 mm) wire (white taped) cut into thirds
- Blossom cutter
- Celstick
- Ball tool
- Toothpick
- General leaf cutter or bramble leaf template (see page 138)
- General leaf veiner
- Posy pick

Makes two flowers and three leaves
- 1 oz (30 g) gum paste
- Red petal dust
- Red paste color
- Green paste color
- Green petal dust
- Silver snowflake petal dust (optional)

Inedible flower

If you prefer, rather than a ball at the base of the flower, you could use a star-shaped sepal, as shown on the finished cake.

1 2 3 4 5 8 9 10 11 14 15 16

To create a stem of fuchsias, take 4 in. (10 cm) of red floral tape, and cut into three lengthwise. Use one thinner strip at a time and taking a full length of 24-gauge (0.5 mm) wire, tape the flower to the wire, adding a new flower every ¾ in. (2 cm).

Tools & Materials
- Basic gum paste tool kit (see page 14)
- 24-gauge (0.5 mm) wire cut into thirds
- At least 20 black cotton stamens per flower
- Floral tape (white and Nile green)
- Celstick
- Stephanotis or jasmine or star cutter
- Ball tool
- Posy pick

Makes one spray
- 1 oz (30 g) gum paste
- Blue paste color
- Green paste color
- Green petal dust

Inedible flower

INTERMEDIATE

34 # Cornflower

A deep blue flower that looks so striking with the contrasting green leaf, which is not as complicated to make as you may think.

1 Take a strand of wire, bend over a small hook at one end, and attach a stamen using white floral tape.

2 Color ¾ oz (22 g) of the paste blue and the remainder green. Take a hazelnut-size ball of blue paste and create a flower using the Mexican hat method (see page 24).

3 Roll the flat part of the flower with the Celstick to thin it, then thread the cutter over the raised center and cut out the petals.

4 Hold the flower in your hand and indent the center with the flower veining tool, then draw the tool up from the center to part way up each petal, indenting the flower as you go and making the center larger.

5 Thread the hooked wire through the center of the flower, concealing it within the flower.

6 Leave the flower to dry—either upright or hanging upside down.

7 Make the leaf by rolling out a hazelnut-size ball of green paste to a thickness of ⅓₂ in. (1 mm), then use the X-acto knife to cut a rectangle of ½ x 1½ in. (1 x 4 cm). Shape one end into an oval and the other to a point. Push a 24-gauge (0.5 mm) wire three-quarters of the way down the length of the leaf.

8 Place the shape on the foam pad, softening the edges using the ball tool, then score the leaf with the flower veining tool to texture. Bend the top over slightly to give a natural appearance. Dust with the green petal dust.

9 Make more flowers and leaves in the same way.

10 Take a central stem of wire and tape with Nile green floral tape.

11 Attach the stamens to the top of the stem with Nile green floral tape, then tape the flowers around this at intervals.

12 Pull out the stamens in the center in a random way, then attach the leaves at the base of the flower with Nile green floral tape. Insert the posy pick into the cake, then insert the flower into this.

Tools & Materials

- Basic gum paste tool kit (see page 14)
- Daphne cutter
- Celstick
- 24-gauge (0.5 mm) wire cut into thirds
- Leaf template (see page 139)
- Floral tape (Nile green)
- Bone tool
- Posy pick

Makes one spray
- 1 oz (30 g) gum paste
- Lilac paste color
- Green paste color
- Green petal dust
- Silver snowflake petal dust (optional)

Inedible flower

Lilac

INTERMEDIATE
35

The beautiful lilac is equally pretty when made in white. The flowers are not difficult to make and the display can be as large or small as is needed.

1 Color three-quarters of the paste with the lilac paste color. Roll a small pinch into a ball, then create one of the flowers using the Mexican hat method (see page 24).

2 Use the Celstick to thin the flattened part, thread the cutter over the raised center, and cut out the shape using the daphne cutter.

3 Hold the flower in your hand and use the pointed end of the flower veining tool to open up the center of the flower.

4 Draw the tool over the petals, softening and thinning them, and use the pointed end of the tool to texture the petals.

5 Take a strand of 24-gauge (0.5 mm) wire, bend a tiny hook in one end, and thread it through the flower center, pulling the little hook into the flower until it disappears. Thin the paste at the base of the flower onto the wire. Make several lilac flowers in the same way.

6 Take another pinch of lilac paste, roll it into a ball, then thread another hooked wire into the ball. Shape the ball into a teardrop, thinning the paste to the wire.

7 Use the X-acto knife to indent a cross at the end of the teardrop to represent the bud petals. Make several buds.

8 Wire all the buds and flowers together, using a thin strand of green floral tape. Start with a few buds, then add in a blossom or two, giving a natural look.

9 Color the remaining paste with the green paste color, then cut out a leaf shape using the template and the X-acto knife. Insert a strand of 24-gauge (0.5 mm) wire up the center of the leaf.

10 Soften the edges of the leaf on the foam pad with the bone tool, then vein the leaf either with a veiner or by hand. Dust the leaf with green petal dust to add a natural appearance.

11 Attach the leaves to the back of the lilac spray with Nile green floral tape, as before. Dust the spray with silver snowflake petal dust if desired. Insert the posy pick into the cake, then insert the flower into this.

1   2   4   4   5   5   9   10

INTERMEDIATE

36

Snowdrop

The snowdrop is one of the first signs of spring. The delicate snowdrops pushing up through the snow can be all shades of green—an array of bobbing heads!

1 Take a length of 24-gauge (0.5 mm) wire and create a small hook on the end.

2 Roll a pea-size ball of paste and thread it down the wire over the hook. Dampen the end of the ball and dip it into the pollen powder.

3 Roll the paste out to a thickness of 1/32 in. (1 mm). Using the cutters, cut two trefoil shapes, one larger than the other. Place on the foam pad.

4 Soften the edges of the shapes with the ball tool, broadening and thinning the paste, then draw the tool up the shape to curl the petals.

5 Thread the smaller petal shape up the wire behind the ball and secure in place with a dot of water.

6 Repeat with the second petal shape.

7 Color the remaining paste green.

8 Take a pea-size ball of paste, roll it into a cone.

Thread the cone down the wire to butt up against the back of the petals. Secure with water.

9 Tape the wire with Nile green floral tape, then bend over the wire approximately 1/2 in. (1 cm) down from the head to give the snowdrop shape.

10 Take another pinch of green paste and shape it into a second cone. Attach it to the wire at the bend, using water.

11 Roll the remaining green paste to a thickness

of 1/8 in. (3 mm), then cut three elongated leaves using the X-acto knife and the template.

12 Thread a 24-gauge (0.5 mm) wire up the center of each leaf, then place on the foam pad and soften the edges with the ball tool. Use the flower veining tool to texture the leaf. Bend the leaf into a natural pose.

13 Wire the leaves to the flower using stem tape. Insert the posy pick into the cake, then insert the flower into this.

If you prefer, the sepal can be made from floral tape in the same shape as the paste sepal.

Tools & Materials

- Basic gum paste tool kit (see page 14)
- Stamens (one per flower)
- 24-gauge (0.5 mm) wire
- Floral tape (white)
- Celstick or toothpick
- Stephanotis or jasmine or medium star cutter
- Small star cutter
- Ball tool

Makes one flower, one leaf, and two buds
- 1 oz (30 g) gum paste
- Pink petal dust
- Silver snowflake petal dust
- Green petal dust
- Green paste color

Inedible flower

INTERMEDIATE
37

Stephanotis

Stephanotis floribunda is an evergreen twining vine originally from Madagascar, loved for its intensely fragrant white flowers that are traditionally used in wedding bouquets.

1 Attach a stamen to a 24-gauge (0.5 mm) wire using white floral tape.

2 Take a hazelnut-size ball of paste, roll it into a ball, and create one of the flowers using the Mexican hat method (see page 24).

3 Roll the flat part of the flower with the Celstick to thin the paste, then thread the cutter over the raised center and cut out the petals.

4 Hold the flower in your hand and indent the center with the flower veining tool, then draw the tool up from the center to part way up each petal, indenting the flower as you go and making the center larger.

5 Thread the stamen through this center—but before it goes into the flower, dampen the stamen and then pull it into the flower to secure.

6 Leave the flower to dry for 10 minutes, then accentuate the center and the base of the flower with pink petal dust, and dust with silver snowflake petal dust.

7 Color ⅓ oz (10 g) paste with green paste color.

Pinch off a pea-size ball, roll out to a thickness of ¹⁄₃₂–¹⁄₁₆ in. (1–2 mm). Cut out a five-pointed star.

8 Place the star on the foam pad and soften the edges with a ball tool, then thread up the back of the stephanotis flower, securing in place with a dot of water.

9 Make the leaf by rolling out more green paste, then cut a rectangle shape with the X-acto knife and shape one short end to a point. Push a 24-gauge (0.5 mm) wire three-quarters of the way down the leaf's length.

10 Place the shape on the foam pad and soften the edges using the ball tool, then score the leaf with the flower veining tool to texture. Bend the leaf into a natural shape. Dust with the green petal dust to naturalize.

11 Shape the bud by rolling a pea-size pinch of paste to an oval shape, narrower at one end. Take a length of 24-gauge (0.5 mm) wire and make a small hook on the end. Insert the wire through the bud, pulling the hook into the paste. Reshape the end, then use the X-acto knife to score the top with a cross to represent the tightly closed petals.

12 Roll out the remaining white paste into a ribbon shape, approximately 2½ in. (6 cm) long and ½ in. (13 mm) wide. Trim the edges with the X-acto knife. Indent the edge of the ribbon with the flower veining tool and make a neat row of dots to add interest. Fold the ends of the ribbon to the center of the ribbon, turn over, and pinch the center. Use the remnants to make another small ribbon to wrap around the center.

1   2   3   5   6   11   11   7   8   9

Tools & Materials

- Basic gum paste tool kit (see page 14)
- Rose petal cutters or template (see page 136)
- Toothpick
- Ball tool
- Rolled-up paper towel

Makes one flower and one leaf
- 1 oz (30 g) gum paste
- Yellow petal dust
- Green paste color

Frangipani

EASY
38

Nothing evokes that tropical feeling quite like the frangipani—their sweet scent and sheer beauty make them universally loved and the blooms look sensational.

1 Roll out three-quarters of the paste to a thickness of ¹⁄₁₆ in. (2 mm).

2 Cut out five petal shapes and place on the foam pad.

3 Use the ball tool to soften the center of the petals, but leave the outer edge of the petals thicker.

4 Use the toothpick to texture the petals by rolling it backward and forward over the petal.

5 Lay the petals out next to each other, then moisten the lower edge of each petal with water.

6 Overlap each petal in a fan shape, with the central points of the petals together.

7 Place on the work board and support using a rolled-up paper towel. Leave to firm up.

8 Color the remaining paste with the green paste color, cut out the leaf using the petal cutter, then place on the foam pad and soften the edges with the ball tool.

9 Texture the leaf with the flower veining tool, position next to the flower, and support with rolled-up paper towel until dry.

10 When dry, dust the center of the flower using the yellow petal dust.

EASY
39 Gerbera

The gerbera comes from the sunflower family, and flowers can be white, yellow, orange, red, and pink, so you can experiment with color schemes. The center of the flower is sometimes black.

1 Color 1¼ oz (40 g) gum paste with the orange paste color.

2 Roll out the paste to a thickness of ⅛ in. (2 mm), and cut out two of each size of daisy cutter. Work quickly to avoid the paste drying out and cracking.

3 Place the shapes on the foam pad and soften the edges of the petals using the ball tool. Enlarge the centers of the two larger shapes by rolling the ball tool over the center. Draw the flower veining tool up the center of each petal to texture.

4 Secure one petal on top of the other using a dot of water. Offset the petals and tweak them using the flower veining tool.

5 Continue building up the flower with two shapes of each size until you have a stack of six shapes.

6 Take a hazelnut-size ball of orange gum paste and flatten to make the flower center. Prick and pull the paste with the toothpick. Dampen lightly with water and dust with the pollen powder.

7 Cut out one of the smallest daisy shapes and prepare as before.

8 Dampen the shape with water, then wrap this around the center that has just been prepared, so the petals curl up the sides.

9 Place this center on the center of the prepared stack of daisy shapes, securing with water. Press into the center, and the other petals will then curl around it.

10 Dampen the center of the flower with water and dust with the pollen powder.

11 Color the remaining paste green for the leaf.

12 Use the leaf cutter to cut out the gerbera leaf Place it on the foam pad, soften the edges with the ball tool, attach to the back of the flower, and support until dry.

Tools & Materials

- Basic gum paste tool kit (see page 14)
- Daisy cutters (extra large, large, and medium)
- Chrysanthemum leaf cutter
- Ball tool
- Toothpick

Makes one flower and one leaf
- 1¾ oz (50 g) gum paste
- Orange paste color
- Green paste color
- Orange pollen powder

2   2   4   5   6   6   8   12   12

The gerbera can
be simplified with
fewer petals to
give pretty,
smaller versions.

Tools & Materials
- Basic gum paste tool kit (see page 14)
- Bone tool
- Toothpick
- Stamens
- Floral tape (green)
- 24-gauge (0.5 mm) wire
- Circle cutter or holly leaf cutter
- Eight-petal daisy cutters (medium and small)
- Five-petal daisy cutter
- Posy pick

Makes one flower and one leaf
- 1 oz (30 g) gum paste
- Purple paste color
- Green paste color
- Green petal dust

Inedible flower

ADVANCED

40 Thistle

The emblem of Scotland—this is a simplified way of making a very complex flower.

1 Take a length of 24-gauge (0.5 mm) wire and bend over the top.

2 Color two-thirds of the paste with the purple paste color. Take a pea-size pinch and shape into a cone. Thread this down the wire, pull the hook into the paste, and shape back into a cone. Prick the top of the cone with the toothpick to texture.

3 Roll out the purple paste to a thickness of ⅛ in. (3 mm) and cut out a strip ½ x 4 in.

(1 x 10 cm). Using the X-acto knife, cut at right angles along one length of the paste to create a fringe. Cut three-quarters of the way through the width of the paste.

4 Dampen the last quarter of the strip with water, then wrap it around the central cone, working all the way around two to three times to build up the shape of the thistle.

5 Color the remaining paste with green paste

color and take a pea-size ball of green paste. Thread it up the wire behind the thistle head.

6 Cut out one five-petal and two eight-petal daisy shapes and place the shapes on the foam pad.

7 Use the bone tool to soften around the daisy petals, drawing the tool up the center of the petals.

8 Dampen the five-petal shape with water, then thread this up the wire behind the thistle and

attach onto the green base, covering the join. Follow this with the two eight-petal daisy shapes, starting with the smaller daisy, making sure that the petal tips are offset.

9 Use the green petal dust to dust the base of the thistle.

10 Roll out the remaining green paste and cut out the leaf using the holly leaf cutter or use a circle cutter to cut out small semicircles up and down each side to create a

spiky holly-leaf effect. Insert a wire through the leaf's center.

11 Use the flower veining tool to vein the leaf and then bend it into a natural position.

12 Dust the leaf with green petal dust and attach to the thistle using floral tape. Insert the posy pick into the cake, then insert the flower into this.

Tools & Materials

- Basic gum paste tool kit (see page 14)
- Kusudama cutter (see page 140)
- Ball tool
- Rolled-up paper towel
- Toothpick

Makes one five-petal flower
- 1 oz (30 g) gum paste
- Black paste color (optional)
- Silver snowflake petal dust (optional)

Origami Kusudama

INTERMEDIATE
41

This design is modeled on the origami kusudama flower made by paper folding.

1 Color the paste lightly with the black paste color to give a light gray color—or leave it white if you prefer.

2 Roll out a hazelnut-size ball of the paste to a thickness of 1/32 in. (1 mm) and cut out one shape with the cutter. Work quickly, as the paste won't fold without cracking when dry.

3 Place the shape on the foam pad and soften the edges using the ball tool.

4 Fold the two triangular wings of the shape toward the center of the shape. Crease the central point at the base of the shape neatly.

5 Curl the shape into a cone and allow to dry for a few minutes in position.

6 Make either another four petals in the same way for the five-petal flower or another three for the four-petal flower.

7 Join them together at the center, using water to secure in place. Hold them in your hand and tweak the flower into a suitable position. Use the rolled-up paper towel to support if necessary.

8 Once dry, take a pea-size ball of paste, roll It into a ball, and flatten with the rolling pin to create a disk.

9 Use the toothpick to frill the edge of the disk and attach to the center of the flower.

10 Take another pea-size ball of paste, flatten it slightly, and prick all over

the surface with the toothpick. Attach to the center of the flower with water.

11 Dust with silver snowflake petal dust if desired.

INTERMEDIATE

42 Hibiscus

The hibiscus flower loves warm weather—a perfect flower on the perfect cake for a summer party!

1 Attach a few stamens to the end of a 24-gauge (0.5 mm) wire using red floral tape, then work down the wire attaching more stamens, until a length of approximately ⅝ in. (1.5 cm) has been covered.

2 Paint the stamens and the floral tape with red pollen powder and leave to dry.

3 Dampen the end of each stamen with water, then dust over with yellow pollen powder for the pollen effect. Leave to dry for 10 minutes.

4 Color three-quarters of the gum paste with the pink paste color and roll out to a thickness of ⅟₃₂ in. (1 mm). Cut out five rose-petal shapes and place on the foam pad.

5 Working quickly, soften the edge of the petal with the bone tool, insert a third of a strand of 24-gauge (0.5 mm) wire, frill the edges a little using the bone tool, and then texture the petal either with a veiner or by hand using the flower veining tool. Curl the petals on the rolled-up paper towel and leave to dry.

6 Dust the center of the petals with the red petal dust to create a deep shade of red in the center of the flower, then blend up the petal. Add in pink dust to further blend the red, finishing with a dusting of silver snowflake petal dust to give a sparkle.

7 Attach the petals to the central stamen, allowing the stamen to stick out quite prominently, using thin strands of floral tape.

8 Color the remaining gum paste with green paste color and roll out to a thickness of ⅟₁₆ in. (2 mm). Using the cutter, cut out a heart shape measuring 1½ x ¾ in. (4 x 2 cm). Insert a third of a length of 24-gauge (0.5 mm) wire up the center of the leaf, stopping three-quarters of the way up.

9 Place the leaf on the foam pad and soften using the ball tool, then score the leaf with the flower veining tool to texture or use the leaf veiner if available. Bend the top over slightly to give a natural appearance.

10 Dust the leaf with the green petal dust and attach to the stem of the flower with floral tape. Insert the posy pick into the cake, then insert the flowers into this.

Tools & Materials

- Basic gum paste tool kit (see page 14)
- Stamens (10 per flower)
- 24-gauge (0.5 mm) wire
- Floral tape (red)
- Rose petal cutter or template (see page 136)
- Bone tool
- Hibiscus veiner (or vein by hand)
- Paper towel
- Heart cutter (see page 138)
- General leaf veiner (or vein by hand)
- Posy pick

Makes one flower and three leaves

- 1 oz (30 g) gum paste
- Red pollen powder
- Yellow pollen powder
- Pink paste color
- Red petal dust
- Pink petal dust
- Silver snowflake petal dust
- Green paste color
- Green petal dust

Inedible flower

1 2 4 5 6 8 9 9 10

Tools & Materials

- Basic gum paste tool kit (see page 14)
- Blossom cutter (small)
- Ball tool
- 24- and 28-gauge (0.5 and 0.3 mm) wire
- Floral tape (Nile green)

Makes 25–30 flowers and three leaves
- 1 oz (30 g) gum paste
- Green petal dust

EASY
43 Lily of the Valley

This is a very delicate-looking flower for spring cakes. It is easy to make using this method and gives a professional finish.

Inedible flower

1 Roll out several pea-size balls of gum paste. You need one for each flower and around seven flowers per stem. Attach to 1½ in. (4 cm) of 28-gauge (0.3 mm) wire by bending the end over and threading the ball down to the bend. Reshape each ball and let dry for 30 minutes.

2 Repeat the first step but with several bigger balls.

3 Roll out a hazelnut-size ball of the white gum paste to a thickness of ⅟₃₂ in. (1 mm). Cut out a blossom for every prepared ball.

4 Place on the foam pad and soften the edges of the blossom with the ball tool. Press the tool into the center of the blossom, and pick up the flower.

5 Dampen the end of the larger balls and press the blossom onto it, indenting the center of the blossom to give the characteristic lily of the valley appearance then bend over the head.

6 Wire the flowers and buds together, using thin strands of Nile green floral tape to make the stalks of lily of the valley.

7 Color ½ oz (15 g) of gum paste with green paste color for the leaves.

8 Roll the paste out to a thickness of ⅛ in. (3 mm) and, using the X-acto knife, cut out an elliptical shape. Thread a 24-gauge (0.5 mm) wire up the center of the leaf, then place on the foam pad and use the ball tool to soften the edges.

9 Use the flower veining tool to score the leaf to give texture. Bend into a natural position and attach to the flower stems using floral tape. Leave to dry.

10 Dust with green petal dust to give a natural appearance. Make two more leaves in the same way and attach to the flower stems using Nile green floral tape.

Tools & Materials

- Basic gum paste tool kit (see page 14)
- 24-gauge (0.5 mm) wire
- Red cotton stamens (four or five per flower)
- Floral tape (green)
- Celstick
- Five-petal daisy cutter (medium)
- Bone tool
- Star cutter
- General leaf cutter or fuchsia leaf template (see page 138)
- General leaf veiner
- Posy pick

Makes five flowers and three leaves
- 1 oz (30 g) gum paste
- Pink paste color
- Green paste color
- Green petal dust

Inedible flower

Florida Azalea

INTERMEDIATE
44

These flowers are best suited to North and Central Florida gardens and come in a number of varieties. Enjoy making your favorite.

1 Tape four or five stamens onto one-third of a strand of 24-gauge (0.5 mm) wire, using floral tape. Allow one of the stamens to protrude farther than the others.

2 Color two-thirds of the gum paste with the pink paste color.

3 Take a hazelnut-size ball of gum paste, roll, and create the flower using the Mexican hat method (see page 24). Roll the flat part of the flower with the Celstick to thin.

Thread the five-petal daisy cutter down over the raised center and cut out the petals.

4 Hold the flower in your hand and indent the center with the flower veining tool, then draw the tool up from the center to part way up each petal, indenting the flower.

5 Turn the flower upside down on the foam pad and draw the ball tool up each petal, curling them back as you work.

6 Thread the prepared stamens through the center of the flower until the stamens are positioned correctly. Pinch the wire to the base of the flower and smooth until it is flush with the wire to make a neat join.

7 Color the remaining paste with green paste color. Roll out a hazelnut-size ball and cut out the star shape with the cutter.

8 Soften the star shape on the foam pad with the bone tool, then thread

it up behind the flower, securing it in place with dots of water.

9 Make four flowers in the same way.

10 Roll out the remaining green paste and cut out the leaf shape.

11 Thread a strand of 24-gauge (0.5 mm) wire up the center of the leaf, then use the general leaf veiner to vein the leaf. Curl into a suitable position and leave to dry for one hour.

12 Dust the leaf with the green petal dust. Make two more leaves.

13 Tape the flowers together in a group, as natural azaleas would be found, adding in the leaves at the back. Use thin strands of floral tape to tape them all together. Insert the posy pick into the cake, then insert the flower into this.

1   3   4   5   6   7   7   10   12

EASY

45 Dogwood

The dogwood is a large, beautiful flower that can be used wired or unwired. It is a simple and elegant flower that looks fabulous on cakes and cupcakes.

1 Roll out a hazelnut-size ball of white paste to a thickness of ⅛ in. (3 mm) and cut out a heart shape using a 1¼ x 1½ in. (3 x 4 cm) cutter.

2 Place on the foam pad. Using the bone tool, soften around the edges of the shape. Work on the top of the petal, broadening the petal and accentuating the indentation of the top.

3 Turn the petal over and soften along the top, curling either side of the indentation back a little.

4 Texture the petal by veining it using the general veiner.

5 Place it back on the foam pad and use the bone tool to frill the edges slightly again. Support on the rolled-up paper towel to dry.

6 Make three more petals in the same way.

7 Dust the petal edges lightly with pink petal dust, then add a slight touch of green in the center, as shown below. Dust with silver snowflake petal dust if desired.

8 Construct the petal on the finished cake by applying a dot of white paste in the desired position dampened with water. Then secure the petal points in position.

9 Color ½ oz (15 g) of paste with pink paste color. Then roll 15 small pink balls in different sizes, but not too big.

10 Gently squash them together into a rough cone shape with a flattened top, then secure this in the center of the petals using water. Dust the flower center with

pink petal dust and silver snowflake dust.

11 Color the remaining white paste with green paste color. Roll out to a thickness of ½₂–⅙ in. (1–2 mm), and cut out two heart-shaped leaves.

12 Place the leaf on the foam pad, soften with the bone tool, then either use the general leaf veiner or the flower veining tool to vein by hand. Tuck the leaf behind the flower and secure as before.

Tools & Materials

- Basic gum paste tool kit (see page 14)
- Heart cutter or template (see page 138)
- Bone tool
- General veiner (or corn-husk veiner, if available)
- Rolled-up paper towel

Makes two flowers
- 1 oz (30 g) gum paste
- Pink petal dust
- Silver snowflake petal dust
- Green petal dust
- Pink paste color
- Green paste color

1   7   9   10   11   12

46 Coiled Fantasy Flower

This is a simple coil that can be rolled easily to create beautiful flowers very quickly. You can frill the edge of the paste to create a variation.

1 Color a pinch of the gum paste with the green paste color and the rest with the pink paste color.

2 Roll out the pink paste to a thickness of ¹⁄₃₂ in. (1 mm), then cut out the coil with the cutter.

3 Start rolling the coil up from the outer end, wrapping it tightly but being careful not to pinch it together. If you want a frilled flower, use the toothpick to soften, thin, and frill the edges before coiling up.

4 Coil up the paste until you have reached the size of flower you need and cut off the remaining paste. If you want a full flower, work right to the end, then twist the central disk under the whole flower to support the coil.

5 Take a toothpick and tweak the petals into a pretty position and leave to dry.

6 Dust with silver snowflake or colored dust to accentuate the petals.

7 Using the green paste, shape into little teardrops, seven in total. Flatten them, then use the flower veining tool to texture the center of the flower.

Tools & Materials

- Basic gum paste tool kit (see page 14)
- Coiled fantasy flower cutter (see page 140)
- Toothpick

Makes three large or six small flowers
- 1 oz (30 g) gum paste
- Green paste color
- Pink paste color
- Pink or silver snowflake petal dust

Tools & Materials

- Basic gum paste tool kit (see page 14)
- Blossom and calyx cutters
- Bone tool
- Toothpick

Makes three flowers
- 1 oz (30 g) gum paste
- Yellow paste color
- Green paste color
- Silver snowflake petal dust (optional)

EASY

47 # Buttercup

The buttercup is an understated flower, but a group of gum paste versions looks beautiful on a spring-themed cake or cupcake.

1 Color two-thirds of the gum paste with yellow paste color.

2 Roll out one-third of the yellow paste to a thickness of 1/32 in. (1 mm) and cut one flower (you need three, but work one at a time).

3 Place the blossom on the foam pad, soften the edges with the bone tool, and then frill slightly.

4 Turn the flower upside down and draw the bone tool lightly up the back of each petal from edge to center to give a slight curl.

5 Turn the flower back over and indent the center slightly.

6 Take a small ball of the yellow paste, flatten, and then prick with the toothpick to texture.

7 Attach the flower center to the center of the blossom with water.

8 Color the remaining paste with the green paste color. Roll out to a thickness of 1/32 in. (1 mm) and cut out the calyx.

9 Place this on the foam pad and soften the edges, then attach to the back of the flower, with the points of the calyx between the petals, securing in place with a dot of water.

10 Reroll the green paste, and cut out a diamond shape with the X-acto knife.

11 Cut out the leaf shape by cutting out two triangles from each side, then more smaller triangles of paste at random to give the shredded look.

12 Texture the leaf using the flower veining tool, drawing it down each segment of the leaf.

13 Attach the leaf to the cupcake or cake with a dot of water and place the flower over the top.

14 Dust with silver snowflake petal dust if desired.

2   3   6   6   8   10   11   12

Tools & Materials

- Basic gum paste tool kit (see page 14)
- Ball tool
- Mini palette knife
- Daisy cutter
- Daisy center mold
- Rolled-up paper towel

Makes one flower
- 1⅛ oz (34 g) gum paste
- Yellow paste color
- Silver snowflake petal dust (optional)

Daisy

EASY
48

A delightful flower with striking colors, the daisy works perfectly adorning a cupcake or as a delicate daisy chain on a larger cake. The fresh colors add a vibrant touch to any summertime celebration cake.

1 Color ⅛ oz (4 g) of the gum paste with yellow paste color and set aside for the daisy center. Roll out the remaining paste to a thickness of ⅛ in. (3 mm).

2 Cut out a daisy and place it on the foam pad. Soften the paste by lightly pressing it with the ball tool.

3 Press a little more firmly with the ball tool to flatten the shape, broadening the mid-section of each petal. Draw the broad end of the flower veining tool along each petal to curl the edges.

4 Make another daisy shape in the same way.

5 Once you have two completed shapes, glue them together at the center, offsetting the petals.

6 Roll the yellow gum paste from step 1 into

a ball and push it firmly into the daisy center mold or sifter (see page 28). Cut off any excess paste using the mini palette knife.

7 Push the paste out of the mold and attach to the center of the daisy using a dab of water.

8 Leave the finished daisy to dry in the position you want it to hold, supported by a rolled-up paper towel.

9 Dust with silver snowflake petal dust if desired.

2   3   5   6   7

Tools & Materials
- Basic gum paste tool kit (see page 14)
- 26-gauge (0.4 mm) wire
- Floral stamens (nine per cupcake)
- White floral tape
- Hydrangea flower cutter
- Ball tool
- Posy pick

Makes nine flowers
- 1 oz (30 g) gum paste
- Blue paste color
- Green paste color
- Dark blue petal dust

Inedible flower

EASY
49 Hydrangea

Hydrangeas are made up of several small flower heads that work well in gum paste and give a lovely, delicate appearance.

1 Cut a length of 26-gauge (0.4 mm) wire into three equal segments and cut a floral stamen in half.

2 Cut a strip of floral tape in half lengthwise to create thin strips of tape. Attach the stamen to the wire using the tape.

3 Color three-quarters of the paste light blue and the remaining paste green, then roll a tiny ball of light blue gum paste and push the stamen into the ball, securing it with a dot of royal icing.

4 Roll ½ oz (15 g) light blue gum paste to a thickness of ⅛ in. (3 mm). Cut out a flower shape with the hydrangea cutter. Gently press it out onto the foam pad with a paintbrush.

5 Soften the paste by lightly pressing the ball tool onto the flower. Press more firmly to flatten and thin the shape further. Roll and thin the edges, making the petals larger and thinner.

6 Push the stamen right through the center of the flower, down to the blue ball, and secure with a dot of royal icing. Position the flower and leave to dry for 30 minutes. Make several flowers using this method.

7 Once you have eight to ten flower heads, tape them together to form a hydrangea flower. Attach them while some flower heads are still soft to get a more accurate, slightly squashed shape. This gives the hydrangea its compact appearance.

8 Once the flowers have been taped together, add a little dark blue petal dust in the center of some of the flower heads or on some of the petals. Insert the posy pick into the cake, then insert the flowers into this.

9 To make the leaves tucked into the display at right, follow the method for Lily of the Valley on page 96.

1   2   3   3   4   5   9   9

The leaves can be attached to the cupcake with a dot of royal icing or, as here, tucked in between the suspended cupcakes.

EASY

50 Cherry Blossom

Cherry blossoms flower *en masse*, making the trees look like pink clouds. The cherry flower can be made with a single or double blossom—the double blossoms will create a fuller flower.

1 Tape eight to ten stamens to a third of a strand of 24-gauge (0.5 mm) wire, using the green floral tape. Separate the stamens out slightly. They can be white and dusted purple/black or ready bought in the required color.

2 Dampen the stamen heads, then dip into the deep red petal dust to cover the top of the stamen and part of the stamen stem.

3 Roll out a hazelnut-size pinch of white paste to a thickness of 1/16 in. (2 mm), then cut out the blossom shape. Place it on the foam pad and soften the edges with the bone tool. As you soften the petal, it will enlarge a little—run the bone tool around the edge of the petals to frill them.

4 Thread the blossom up behind the prepared stamens, and just before pulling the stamens into the center of the flower, dampen the center. Pinch the blossom around the stamens to secure. Hang the stem upside down until dry.

5 Make some flowers with the petals more curled up and others that are more open. If you curl the petal almost together, add the calyx to the back; this will make the bud.

6 Dust pink on the center of the flower around the base of the stamens.

7 Color 1/3 oz (10 g) of paste with green paste color, take a pea-size ball, and create a calyx using the Mexican hat method (see page 24). Use the Celstick to thin the flat part of the calyx further.

8 Thread the calyx cutter down over the raised center and cut out the calyx.

9 Place on the foam pad and soften slightly.

10 Thread the calyx up behind the flower and secure in place with dots of water.

11 Roll out the remnants of green paste for a leaf, approximately 2 x ¾ in. (5 x 2 cm) and 1/32 in.

(1 mm) thick. Cut out an elliptical shape using the X-acto knife or template.

12 Place the leaf on the foam pad and soften the edges with the bone tool. Thread a third of a strand of 24-gauge (0.5 mm) wire up the center of the leaf. Vein the leaf with either the general veiner or by hand using the flower veining tool.

14 Bend into a suitable position to dry.

15 Dust with the green petal dust to create a realistic-looking leaf.

16 Tape the leaf to the flower stem using floral tape.

The flowers can be made without calyx or leaf for a simpler decoration.

Tools & Materials

- Basic gum paste tool kit (see page 14)
- White cotton thread on a reel
- Clematis petal and leaf cutter or large lily petal template (see page 136) and leaf template (see page 138)
- Clematis petal veiner (or vein by hand)
- General leaf veiner (or vein by hand)
- Bone tool
- Toothpick
- Floral tape (Nile green)
- 24-gauge (0.5 mm) wire
- Posy pick

Makes one flower and one leaf
- 1 oz (30 g) gum paste
- Yellow petal dust
- Pink petal dust
- Silver snowflake petal dust
- Green paste color
- Green petal dust

Inedible flower

EASY
51 # Clematis

The clematis can be found in many amazing colors, so any variety will blend well when putting together a spray of different flowers to decorate a summer garden cake.

1 Take the cotton thread and wind it loosely around two fingers several times. Take it off your fingers and attach a third of a strand of wire with a hook on the end around the center.

2 Bend the threads upward and attach green floral tape over the base of the threads and onto the wire, holding the threads in place. Trim the tops of the threads with scissors.

3 Dust the threads with yellow petal dust, then dampen the ends of the threads and dip into the petal dust to allow it to stick to the threads. Leave to dry.

4 Roll out two-thirds of the gum paste to a thickness of 1⁄16 in. (2 mm). Cut out five clematis petal shapes and place them on the foam pad.

5 Working quickly, soften the edge of the petal with the bone tool, insert a third of a strand of 24-gauge (0.5 mm) wire, frill the edges a little using the bone tool, then texture the petal either with a veiner or by hand using the flower veining tool. Curl the petals as desired and leave to dry.

6 Dust up the center of the petal with the pink dust to create a deep shade of pink, then blend up the petal, getting fainter as you work up, finishing with a dusting of silver snowflake petal dust.

7 Attach the petals to the central stamen using thin strands of floral tape.

8 Color the remaining gum paste with green paste color and roll out to a thickness of 1⁄16 in. (2 mm) Cut out the leaf.

Insert a third of a strand of 24-gauge (0.5 mm) wire three-quarters of the way up the center of the leaf.

9 Place the leaf on the foam pad and soften using the ball tool, then score the leaf with the flower veining tool to texture or use the veiner. Bend the top over slightly to give a natural look.

10 Dust with the green petal dust and attach to the flower. Insert the posy pick into the cake, then insert the flower into this.

If making several
flowers, make your
task easier by leaving
out the leaves.

Buttercream Flowers

Coiled Rose

Tools & Materials
- Piping bag
- Star decorating tip
- Small palette knife

Makes 12 flowers
- Quantity of natural-colored buttercream (see page 18)
- Red paste color

A quick and simple way to cover and decorate a cupcake in one go! Use a block-colored buttercream or try this two-tone effect.

1 In this example, the flower is piped onto a fondant disk. Prepare the piping bag (see page 20) and insert the star tip.

2 Using the palette knife, paint red paste color thinly down the inside of one side of the bag. Fill the bag with natural-colored buttercream. This will create the two-tone effect.

3 In one continuous movement, start piping in the center of the cake or cupcake, then pipe around in a coil shape. Continue until the flower is the desired size.

EASY
53 Rose

A stiffer buttercream gives the frilled edges to the petals, whereas a buttercream that is softer will give a broader petal.

1 In this example, the flower is piped onto a fondant disk. Color the buttercream with the red paste color. Prepare the piping bag (see page 20) and insert the tip.

2 To make a softer buttercream, a dash of milk, water, or a flavoring such as orange juice or vanilla essence can be added sparingly. If too much liquid is added, thicken the mixture by adding more confectioner's sugar.

3 Pipe a cone in the center of the cake or cupcake for the center of the rose.

4 Pipe two semicircular shapes around the cone, angling the tip straight upright.

5 Pipe three semicircular shapes on the next row, angling the top of the tip slightly outward.

6 Pipe five petals on the next row.

7 Continue building up the flower with petals until it is the required size.

Tools & Materials
- Piping bag
- Wilton decorating tip no. 104
- Small palette knife

Makes 12 flowers
- Quantity of natural-colored buttercream (see page 18)
- Red paste color

3   4   5   6   7

Carnation

A side view of a carnation is a useful flower to add to a repertoire of buttercream flowers for designs on the sides of large cakes.

Tools & Materials

- Piping bags x 2
- Wilton decorating tips no. 104 and no. 3
- Small palette knife

Makes 12 flowers
- Half the quantity of natural-colored buttercream (see page 18)
- Red paste color
- Green paste color

1 In this example, the flower is piped onto a fondant disk. Prepare the piping bag (see page 20) and insert the no. 104 tip.

2 Color a tablespoon of the buttercream with the red paste color. Using the small palette knife, smear the red paste down the side of the piping bag, ensuring that the line corresponds with the broad end of the decorating tip. Fill the bag with half of the remaining buttercream.

3 Hold the decorating tip with the narrow end against the cake surface, then pipe in a ruffle effect (a neat zigzag) in an arc shape.

4 Pipe two more rows under the first, overlapping with the previous row and making each row shorter.

5 Prepare the other piping bag and insert the no. 3 tip. Color the remaining buttercream with the green paste color and fill the piping bag. Pipe the stalk and a leaf in neat zigzags.

Tools & Materials

- Piping bags x 2
- Wilton decorating tips no. 104 and no. 3
- Small palette knife
- Toothpick

Makes 12 flowers
- Half the quantity of natural-colored buttercream (see page 18)
- Yellow paste color
- Blue paste color

INTERMEDIATE

55

Pansy

Choose your favorite colors and pipe a buttercream pansy onto a cupcake for an immediate winner.

1 In this example, the flower is piped onto a fondant disk. Color half the buttercream yellow and half the buttercream blue (or the colors you have chosen). Prepare the piping bag (see page 20), insert the no. 104 tip, and fill with yellow buttercream.

2 Pipe two fan shapes close together on the top of the cake or cupcake. Do this by holding the narrow end of the tip on the cake surface and twisting the tip around in an arc, pivoting on the narrow end while squeezing the bag.

3 Repeat this process with two more fan shapes slightly lower and in front of the first two.

4 Prepare the other piping bag, insert the no. 104 tip, and fill with blue buttercream.

5 Hold the narrow end of the tip to the base of the yellow buttercream fans, then pipe a fan shape with the blue buttercream. Squeeze the bag firmly to get a good flow of buttercream and a more frilled effect.

6 Finish the flower by using a small amount of yellow buttercream in a bag with the no. 3 tip and piping a circle in the center of the flower.

7 If necessary, use a toothpick to neaten the center of the flower.

2

3

5

Tools & Materials

- Piping bags x 3
- Wilton decorating tips 2 x no. 113 and 1 x no. 3
- Small palette knife

Makes 12 flowers
- Quantity of natural-colored buttercream (see page 18)
- Red paste color
- Green paste color

Poinsettia EASY 56

The Christmas poinsettia, a perfect flower to pipe onto a spicy cinnamon cupcake.

1 In this example, the flower is piped onto a fondant disk. Color two dessertspoons of buttercream with the red color and two dessertspoons with the green color.

2 Prepare two piping bags (see page 20) and insert the no. 113 tips.

3 Fill one piping bag with the red buttercream and the other piping bag with the green buttercream.

4 Start piping the red bracts on the outside edge of the flower in a circular shape.

5 The bracts are formed by holding the bag at a 45-degree angle to the cake or cupcake surface, with the flat of the tip resting on the cake surface. Start squeezing the piping bag while drawing the tip up and away from the cake or cupcake. Stop squeezing and pull the bag away to create the bract.

6 Using the same piping techniques as for the bracts, on the first row, pipe a few green leaves intermingled in the red bracts.

7 Start a row of bracts on the inside of the first, continuing until the whole flower is filled with bracts.

8 Prepare the third piping bag, insert the no. 3 tip, and fill with the remaining green buttercream.

9 Pipe dots in the center of the flower.

ADVANCED
57 Chrysanthemum

This flower is well worth the effort in trying to master the technique. Once mastered, it is effective for lots of flowers with tiny clusters of petals.

1 In this example, the flower is piped onto a fondant disk. Color the buttercream with the purple paste color.

2 Prepare the piping bag (see page 20) and insert the tip.

3 Fill the piping bag with the purple buttercream.

4 Pipe the outside edge of the flower on the cake's surface, in a circular shape made up of short petals.

5 The petals are formed by holding the bag at a 45-degree angle to the cake or cupcake surface, with the center of the horseshoe-shaped tip resting on the surface. Start squeezing the piping bag while drawing the tip up and away from the cake or cupcake. Stop squeezing and pull the bag away to create the petal.

6 Continue all the way around the flower, creating a circle of petals, then start a row on the inside of the first, continuing and building up the petals to create the flower.

7 If you make a mistake or are not happy with the effect, simply scrape the buttercream off the cake with a palette knife and start again!

4

6

6

Tools & Materials

- Piping bags x 2
- Wilton decorating tips no. 104 and no. 3
- Small palette knife

Makes 12 flowers
- Half the quantity of natural-colored buttercream (see page 18)
- Yellow paste color

Daisy

EASY
58

An easy flower for a beginner to pipe, good as a single flower on a cake or as several flowers piped together.

1 In this example, the flower is piped onto a fondant disk. Prepare the piping bag (see page 20) and insert the no. 104 tip.

2 Fill the piping bag with three-quarters of the natural buttercream (color it purple if you'd like to make Michaelmas daisies).

3 Pipe the first petal by placing the narrow end of

the decorating tip on the cupcake or cake surface. Squeeze the bag while drawing the large end of the tip up and down in an "n"-shape. This will create the petal. Make the shape very narrow to emulate the shape of a daisy petal.

4 Repeat this process seven more times to create an eight-petal flower, making sure that

the center of each petal is at the same point.

5 Color the remaining buttercream with the yellow paste color. Prepare the other piping bag, insert the no. 3 tip, and add the yellow buttercream. Pipe a small coil first, then pipe dots on top of the coil for the flower center.

Tools & Materials

- Piping bags x 2
- Wilton decorating tips no. 104 and no. 3
- Small palette knife
- Toothpick

Makes 12 flowers
- Quantity of natural-colored buttercream (see page 18)
- Yellow paste color

INTERMEDIATE

59

Daffodil

Spring is here when daffodils appear—freshly baked cupcakes with a daffodil head on each, so inspiring!

1 In this example, the flower is piped onto a fondant disk. Color the buttercream with the yellow paste color.

2 Prepare the piping bag (see page 20), insert the no. 104 tip, and fill with three-quarters of the yellow buttercream.

3 Pipe the first petal by placing the narrow end of the decorating tip on the cake surface. Squeeze the bag while drawing the large end up and down in an "n"-shape. This will create the petal shape. Make the shape narrow.

4 Repeat this process four more times to create a five-petal flower, making sure that the center of each petal is at the same point.

5 Prepare the other bag, insert the no. 3 tip, and fill with the remaining yellow buttercream.

6 Pipe a small ring around the center of the petals. Continue piping over the same ring several times to build up for the trumpet of the flower.

7 Take the toothpick and lightly pull out the final ring just piped to give a frilled edge.

3   4   6   7

Tools & Materials

- Piping bags x 2
- Wilton decorating tip no. 3
- Small palette knife

Makes 12 flowers
- Half the quantity of natural-colored buttercream (see page 18)
- Pale green paste color
- Purple paste color

Bluebell

EASY **60**

A delicate nodding flower that would look perfect on the side of a cake with other bluebells in a row.

Backward-facing "s"
Teardrop shape
"S" shape

1 Color half of the buttercream pale green and half purple.

2 Prepare the piping bag (see page 20), insert the no. 3 tip, and fill with the purple buttercream. The flower is made up of three piped petals. Pipe the first petal in an elongated "s" shape. Pipe the middle petal by piping a thick teardrop. Finish the flower by piping the third petal as a backward "s," so that it mirrors the first petal.

3 Pipe through the center of the two shapes, giving depth to the center of the flower.

4 Prepare the other piping bag, insert the no. 3 tip, and fill with the green buttercream. Pipe the sepal on the flower, then the stalk, and finally a leaf.

Tools & Materials

- Piping bags x 2
- Wilton decorating tips no. 104 and no. 3
- Small palette knife

Makes 12 flowers
- Quantity of natural-colored buttercream (see page 18)
- Purple paste color
- Green paste color

INTERMEDIATE

61 Sweet Pea

String groups of sweet peas together on the side of a cake for a quick but effective decoration.

1 In this example, the flower is piped onto a fondant disk. Prepare the piping bag (see page 20) and insert the no. 104 tip.

2 Using the small palette knife, smear a small amount of the purple paste color down the side of the piping bag, ensuring that the line corresponds with the broad end of the decorating tip.

3 Fill the piping bag with three-quarters of the natural buttercream.

4 Hold the piping tip with the narrow end against the cake surface, squeeze the bag, and draw the tip around in a semicircle—this will create a fan shape with a dark purple edge.

5 Repeat the previous step to overlay a second petal; however, move the tip down by ¼ in. (6 mm) to allow the petal to be piped slightly lower than the first.

6 Color the remaining buttercream with the green paste color. Prepare the other piping bag, insert the no. 3 tip, and add the green buttercream.

7 Pipe the sepal and stalk, with a little leaf to finish.

4

5

7

Tools & Materials

- Piping bags x 2
- Wilton decorating tips no. 104 and no. 3
- Small palette knife

Makes 36 flowers
- Quantity of natural-colored buttercream (see page 18)
- Pink paste color
- Yellow paste color

4

5

6

Apple Blossom

INTERMEDIATE

62

Put clusters of three apple blossoms on each cupcake, overlapping their petals.

1 In this example, the flower is piped onto a fondant disk. Prepare the piping bag (see page 20) and insert the no. 104 tip.

2 Using the small palette knife, smear a small amount of the pink paste color down the side of the piping bag, ensuring that the line corresponds with the broad end of the decorating tip.

3 Fill the piping bag with all but two dessertspoons of natural buttercream.

4 Pipe the first petal by placing the narrow end of the decorating tip on the cake surface. Squeeze the bag while drawing the large end up and down in an "n"-shape. This will create the petal.

5 Repeat this process four times to create a five-petal flower, making sure that the center of each petal is at the same point.

6 Color the remaining buttercream with the yellow paste color. Prepare the other piping bag, insert the no. 3 tip, and add the yellow buttercream. Pipe dots in the center.

Tools & Materials
- Piping bags x 2
- Wilton decorating tips no. 104 and no. 3
- Toothpick
- Small palette knife

Makes 12 flowers
- Quantity of natural-colored buttercream (see page 18)
- Red paste color
- Black paste color
- Black nonpareils (optional)

EASY
63 Poppy

A striking red flower with black nonpareils sprinkled in the center to form the whorl of stamens.

1 In this example, the flower is piped onto a fondant disk. Color all but three tablespoons of buttercream red.

2 Prepare the piping bag (see page 20), insert the no. 104 tip, and fill the piping bag with the red buttercream.

3 Pipe the first petal by placing the narrow end of the decorating tip on the cake surface. Squeeze the bag while drawing the large end up and down in an "n"-shape. This will create the petal shape.

4 Repeat this process four more times to create a five-petal flower, making sure that the center of each petal is at the same point.

5 Color the remaining buttercream with the black paste color. Prepare the other piping bag, insert the no. 3 tip, and add the black buttercream. Fill in the center of the poppy by piping black dots, and if desired, sprinkle with black nonpareils.

Tools & Materials

- Piping bags x 2
- Wilton decorating tips no. 81 and no. 3
- Small palette knife

Makes 12 flowers
- Quantity of natural-colored buttercream (see page 18)
- Brown paste color
- Yellow paste color

Sunflower

To recreate the sunflower requires some skills with a piping bag, but this technique is one that's worth mastering.

1 In this example, the flower is piped onto a fondant disk. Color three tablespoons of the buttercream brown and the rest yellow.

2 Prepare the piping bag (see page 20), insert the no. 81 tip, and fill the piping bag with yellow buttercream.

3 Start piping the outside edge of the flower on the top of the cake or cupcake, in a circular shape made up of short petals.

4 The petals are formed by holding the bag at a 45-degree angle to the cake or cupcake surface, with the center of the horseshoe-shaped tip resting on the surface. Start squeezing the piping bag while drawing the tip up and away from the cake or cupcake. Stop squeezing and pull the bag away to create the petal.

5 Continue all the way around the flower, creating a circle of petals, then start a row on the inside of the first, continuing for three or four rows.

6 Prepare the other piping bag, insert the no. 3 tip, and add the brown buttercream. Pipe thick dots all over the center of the flower.

EASY
65 Lavender

Purple paste color perfectly captures the lovely shade of lavender.

1 In this example, the flower is piped onto a fondant disk. Color all but three dessertspoons of buttercream with the green paste color.

2 Prepare the piping bag (see page 20), insert the no. 3 tip, and fill the piping bag with green buttercream.

3 Pipe long, sweeping green lines on the top of the cupcake or cake. This flower requires a smooth, flat surface.

4 Pipe little green teardrop shapes up the stalk for the random leaves on the lavender stalk.

5 Color the remaining buttercream with the purple paste color. Prepare the other piping bag, insert the no. 3 tip, and add the purple buttercream.

6 Pipe little purple teardrops randomly up the stalks for the lavender flowers.

3   4   6

Tools & Materials
- Piping bags x 2
- Wilton decorating tips no. 104 and no. 3
- Small palette knife

Makes 12 flowers
- Half the quantity of natural-colored buttercream (see page 18)
- Green paste color
- Yellow paste color

Zinnia ADVANCED 66

Zinnias comes in so many colors—try making several different shades for a truly colorful cupcake display.

1 In this example, the flower is piped onto a fondant disk. Color all but two dessertspoons of the buttercream with the green paste color.

2 Prepare the piping bag (see page 20), insert the no. 104 tip, and fill the piping bag with green buttercream.

3 Pipe the first petal by placing the narrow end of the decorating tip on the cake surface. Squeeze the bag while drawing the large end up and down in an "n"-shape. This will create the petal shape.

4 Repeat this process nine times to create a 10-petal flower, making sure that the center of each petal is at the same point.

5 Pipe the next row right on top of the first from the center, making the petals shorter.

6 Create a third row on top of the others, making it shorter still, so that the three layers are clear.

7 Color the remaining buttercream with the yellow paste color. Prepare the other piping bag, insert the no. 3 tip, and add the yellow buttercream. Pipe dots in the center of the flower.

Royal Icing
Flowers

Orchid 67

As well as piping these flowers directly onto the cake, pipe them onto squares of parchment paper. The flowers will then dry and can be applied to any part of the cake by securing with a dot of royal icing.

Tools & Materials

- Piping bag
- Wilton decorating tip no. 104
- Small palette knife
- Paintbrush

Makes 12 flowers
- One-quarter quantity of royal icing (see page 19)
- Pink paste color

1 Color the royal icing with the pink paste color.

2 Prepare the piping bag and insert the no. 104 tip.

3 Using the small palette knife, fill the piping bag with pink royal icing.

4 Pipe the first petal by placing the narrow end of the decorating tip on the cake surface. Squeeze the bag while drawing the broad end up and round in a fan shape.

5 Repeat this process twice more in a triangle shape to create a three-petal shape, making sure that the center of each petal is at the same point.

6 Hold the shape with a petal pointing away from you; the next two petals are going to be piped in between this petal, as shown below.

7 Turn the flower upside down and pipe a fan shape at the base, but make this much fuller. Leave to dry for 24 hours.

8 Use the paintbrush to paint the center of the orchid with pink paste color to accentuate the center of the petals.

4   5   6   7

INTERMEDIATE

68 Wild Rose

The wild rose can be piped in an array of colors. Try piping it in white and dusting the edges in pink to give a delicate appearance.

1 Color the royal icing with the yellow paste color. Prepare the piping bag and insert the no. 103 tip.

2 Using the small palette knife, fill the piping bag with all but two

dessertspoons of the yellow royal icing.

3 Place the tip with the broad end on the piping surface and pipe an "n"-shape while moving the narrow end a little, to create the petal.

4 Pipe four more petals to create the flower.

5 Darken the color of the remaining royal icing by adding more paste color. Fill a piping bag, snip the tip off the bag, and pipe dots into the flower center.

Tools & Materials

- Piping bags x 2
- Wilton decorating tip no. 103
- Small palette knife

Makes 40 flowers
- One-quarter quantity of royal icing (see page 19)
- Yellow paste color

Tools & Materials

* Piping bag
* Wilton decorating tip no. 3
* Rolling pin
* Rose petal cutter
* Small palette knife
* Paintbrush

Makes 12 flowers
* 1 oz (30 g) gum paste
* Peach paste color
* One-quarter quantity of royal icing (see page 19)
* Alcohol (vodka)
* Silver snowflake petal dust

Fantasy Daisy

This is a good flower to start with because the pieces are dried flat and then constructed into the flower.

1 Color the gum paste with peach paste color. Roll out the paste to a thickness of 1/32 in. (1 mm) Use the rose petal cutter to cut out seven petals for the flower and dry them flat.

2 Color all the royal icing with peach paste color.

Prepare the piping bag and insert the no. 3 tip. Using the small palette knife, fill the bag with royal icing. Pipe a line of royal icing around the curved edge of the petal.

3 With a damp paintbrush (dampen with water, but dry a little first—it must not be dripping) and before the royal icing sets, draw the paintbrush through the soft royal icing.

4 Pipe a second line of royal icing a little below the first, repeating the brushing with the damp paintbrush. You can do this two or three times on each petal, depending on the effect you want to create. Leave to dry.

5 Mix a paste using the alcohol and silver snowflake dust. Use the paste to paint the white flecks onto the petals.

6 Pipe a large dot of royal icing where you want the center of the flower to be. Attach the petals in a fan shape, securing in place with royal icing on the back as you work. Pipe a center to the flower. Dust with silver snowflake petal dust if you wish.

1   2   3   5

70 Ox-eye Daisy

A just-picked white daisy with a bright yellow center. Pipe the flower directly into position. If you make a mistake, simply scrape the icing off with a palette knife and start again!

1 Prepare the piping bag and insert the no. 127 tip.

2 Using the small palette knife, fill the piping bag with white royal icing. Reserve a small amount for the flower centers.

3 Pipe the first petal by placing the broad end of the decorating tip on the cake surface. Squeeze the bag while drawing the narrow end up and round in an "n"-shape.

4 Continue working around the flower, one petal at a time, until the whole circle of petals is complete—10 in total.

5 Color the remaining royal icing with the yellow paste color. Fill a piping bag with yellow royal icing, snip the tip off the piping bag, and pipe the dots in the center of the flower.

Tools & Materials

- Piping bags x 2
- Wilton decorating tip no. 127
- Small palette knife

Makes 50 flowers
- One-quarter quantity of royal icing (see page 19)
- Yellow paste color

3   4   4   4   5

Cactus Blossom

EASY
71

Set the cactus blossom against a pastel-colored fondant background to make its subtle charms stand out.

Tools & Materials

- Piping bags x 2
- Wilton decorating tip no. 69
- Small palette knife

Makes 30 flowers
- One-quarter quantity of royal icing (see page 19)

1 Prepare the piping bag and insert the no. 69 tip. Using the small palette knife, fill the piping bag with white royal icing. Reserve a small amount for the flower center.

2 Place the tip on the piping surface and squeeze the bag, at the same time lifting the tip up and out. Stop squeezing and pull the tip away, leaving a petal shape.

3 Continue in the same way, creating a ring of petals.

4 Work another two rows inside the first.

5 Finish the blossom off by filling a bag with the remaining white royal icing, snip the tip off the bag, and pipe dots into the center of the flower.

EASY

72 Flax

An unusual flower to include in a book on sugar flowers, but there are so few blue subjects that this one had to be featured. It's pretty and easy to make.

1 Color all but two tablespoons of the royal icing with the blue paste color. Prepare the piping bag and insert the no. 103 tip.

2 Using the small palette knife, fill the piping bag with blue royal icing.

3 Pipe the first petal by placing the broad end of the decorating tip on the cake surface. Hold the tip quite upright. Squeeze the bag while drawing the narrow end up and round in an n-shape.

4 Continue working around the flower, one petal at a time, until the whole circle of petals is complete—five in total.

5 Color the remaining royal icing with the green paste color. Fill a piping bag with green royal icing, snip the tip off the piping bag, and pipe the dots in the center of the flower.

3   4   4   4   5   5

Tools & Materials

- Piping bags x 2
- Wilton decorating tip no. 103
- Small palette knife

Makes 50 flowers
- One-quarter quantity of royal icing (see page 19)
- Pink paste color
- Yellow paste color
- Silver snowflake petal dust

Alpine Blossom

INTERMEDIATE
73

A crisp, fresh blossom to pipe that requires a little more skill, as the petals overlay each other—but it is definitely worth the effort.

1 Prepare the piping bag and insert the no. 103 tip.

2 Using the small palette knife, smear a small amount of the pink paste color down the side of the piping bag, ensuring that the line corresponds with the narrow end of the decorating tip.

3 Fill the piping bag with white royal icing. Reserve two tablespoons for the flower centers.

4 Pipe the first petal by placing the broad end of the decorating tip on the cake surface. Squeeze the bag while drawing the narrow end up and round in a fan shape.

5 Repeat this process four times to create a five-petal flower, making sure that the center of each petal is at the same point.

6 Color the remaining royal icing with the yellow paste color. Fill a piping bag with yellow royal icing, snip the tip off the piping bag, and pipe the dots in the center of the flower.

7 Dust with silver snowflake petal dust when dry.

4   5   6   6   6

Tools & Materials

- Piping bags x 2
- Wilton decorating tip no. 104
- Small palette knife

Makes 40 flowers
- One-quarter quantity of royal icing (see page 19)
- Yellow paste color

EASY
74 Trillium

A pretty frilled flower, and the frilled effect is easy to create!

1 Prepare the piping bag and insert the no. 104 tip.

2 Using the small palette knife, fill the piping bag with white royal icing. Reserve a small amount for the flower centers.

3 Place the tip with the narrow end on the piping surface and pipe a fan shape, undulating the bag at the same time to get a rippled effect.

4 Pipe two more petals to create a three-petal flower.

5 Color the remaining royal icing with the yellow paste. Fill a piping bag with yellow royal icing, snip the tip off the piping bag, and pipe three large dots in the center of the flower.

3   4   4   5   5

Tools & Materials

- Piping bags x 3
- Wilton decorating tip no. 104
- Small palette knife

Makes 45 flowers
- One-quarter quantity of royal icing (see page 19)
- Purple paste color
- Yellow paste color
- Orange paste color

Viola

INTERMEDIATE
75

If you're not sure of your piping skills, pipe this flower onto a small square of parchment paper and leave to dry. The purple icing will stain whatever it touches and can't be removed.

1 Color half the royal icing with the purple paste color. Prepare the piping bag and insert the no. 104 tip. Using the small palette knife, fill the piping bag with purple royal icing.

2 Place the tip with the broad end on the piping surface and pipe an "n"-shape while moving the narrow end slightly to create the petal. Repeat.

3 Wash the tip. Color the other half of the royal icing with the yellow paste color, reserving a small amount for the flower centers. Prepare a new bag, insert the tip, and fill with yellow royal icing.

4 Pipe two petals either side of the purple petals, using the same technique.

5 Pipe the base petal by placing the narrow end of the tip at the center of the flower and squeezing the piping bag while moving the narrow end of the decorating tip in an "n"-shape, moving the piping bag up and down to get a frilled effect.

6 Color the remaining royal icing with the orange paste color. Fill a piping bag with orange royal icing, snip the tip off the piping bag, and pipe a dot in the flower center.

Templates

If you don't have the specific cutters required, use these templates to create several of the flowers and leaves in the book. Trace the flowers onto cardstock or plastic (for example, ice-cream or margarine containers) and cut the shape out with scissors.

Rose petal
pages 41, 48, 60, 72, 78,
89, 94

Lily petals
pages 43, 66, 80, 108

Mimosa leaf
page 47

Jasmine leaf
page 55

Mistletoe leaf
page 55

Orchid petals
pages 42, 68

Cala lily petal
page 52

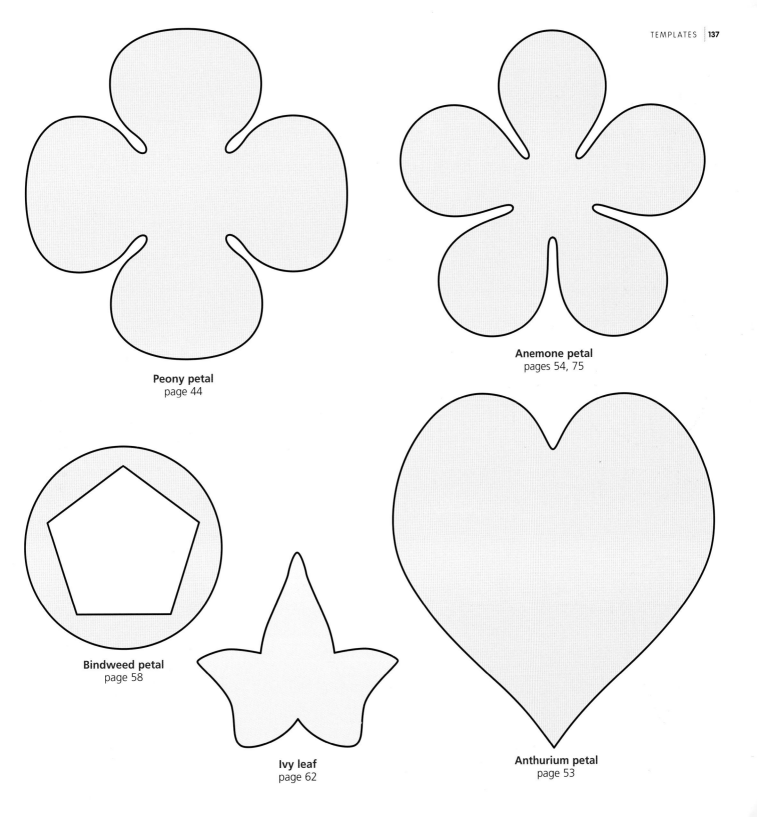

Peony petal
page 44

Anemone petal
pages 54, 75

Bindweed petal
page 58

Ivy leaf
page 62

Anthurium petal
page 53

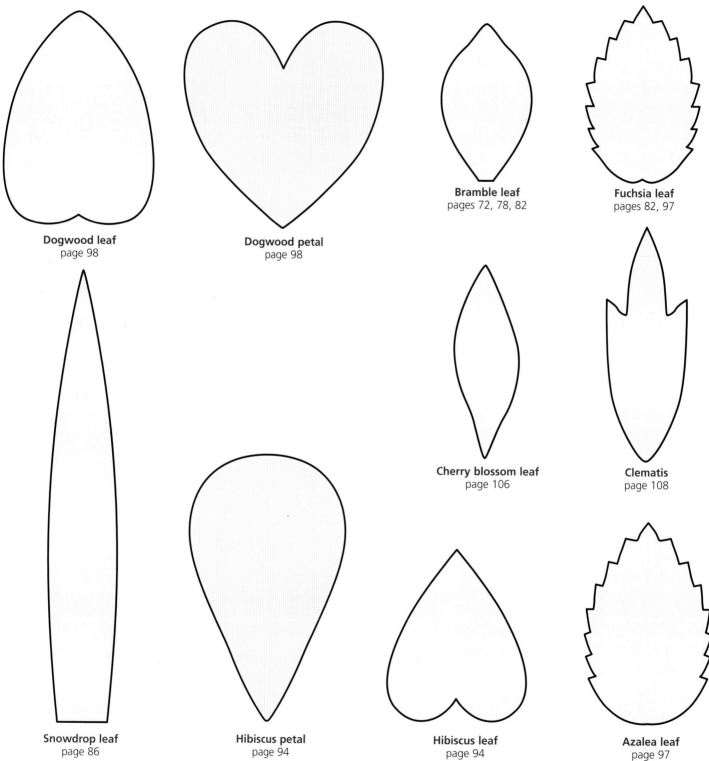

Dogwood leaf
page 98

Dogwood petal
page 98

Bramble leaf
pages 72, 78, 82

Fuchsia leaf
pages 82, 97

Cherry blossom leaf
page 106

Clematis
page 108

Snowdrop leaf
page 86

Hibiscus petal
page 94

Hibiscus leaf
page 94

Azalea leaf
page 97

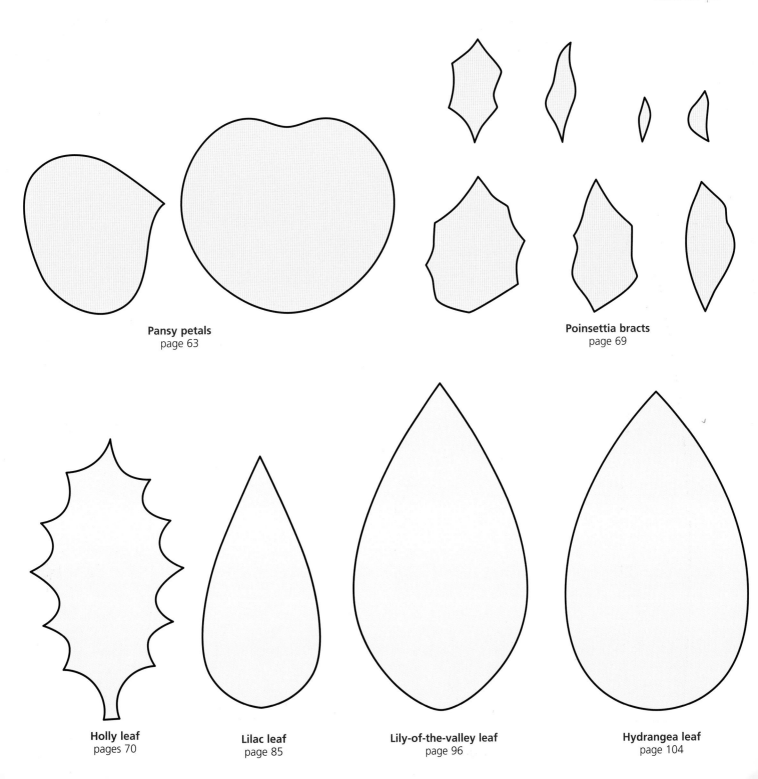

Pansy petals
page 63

Poinsettia bracts
page 69

Holly leaf
pages 70

Lilac leaf
page 85

Lily-of-the-valley leaf
page 96

Hydrangea leaf
page 104

Resources

Squires Kitchen
www.squires-shop.com
International postage available
T: +44 (0)1252 260 260
e: customer@squires-shop.com

Gum paste, royal icing powder, marzipan, modeling chocolate, petal dusts, and paste, liquid, and gel food colors.

Too Nice To Slice
www.toonicetoslice.co.uk
International postage available
T: +44 (0)7880 701732
e: toonicetoslicebyhelenpenman@
gmail.com

Helen Penman cutters (including the kusudama and coil flower cutters), cupcake wrappers, and more available in the Online Store.

Kit Box
www.kitbox.co.uk
T: +44 (0)1275 879 030
e: support@kitbox.info

Metal cutters, ribbon cutters, and general cake-decorating supplies.

CelCakes & CelCrafts
www.celcrafts.com
T: +44 (0)1759 371447
e: sales@celcrafts.com

Cake-decorating tools.

Hawthorne Hill
www.hawthornehill.co.uk
T: +44 (0)7905 811505
e: Via contact form on website.

Orchid and other flower cutters, molds, and tools.

Fancy Flours
www.fancyflours.com
T: +1 (406) 587 0118
e: info@fancyflours.com

General baking supplies.

Wilton
www.wilton.com
T: +1 888 373 4588
e: Via contact form on website.

Cake-decorating tools, cutters, decorating tips, and piping bags.

Index

Acknowledgments

All step-by-step and other images are the copyright of Quarto Publishing plc. While every effort has been made to credit contributors, Quarto would like to apologize should there have been any omissions or errors—and would be pleased to make the appropriate correction for future editions of the book.

Author's acknowledgments

I have been very fortunate that Squires Kitchen in Farnham, Surrey, England, have liked my cake designs over the years and featured them in their magazines, written two books with me, and they also supplied the pastes for the flowers in this book. I am very grateful to Beverley and Jenny at Squires for their support. I have also been so blessed to have such an amazing publishing team at Quarto— Kate, Ruth, and Emma—without whom this book wouldn't be!